My Friend Degas

has been composed in Linotype Baskerville and printed directly from type by Connecticut Printers, Inc., Hartford. The illustrations have been printed by offset lithography by the Meriden Gravure Company, Meriden, Connecticut. The binding has been done by the Vail-Ballou Press, Inc., Binghamton, New York.

Wesleyan University Press
MIDDLETOWN, CONNECTICUT

My Friend Degas

The French edition of M. Halévy's memoir
was published in 1960 by La Palatine, Paris,
under the title *Degas parle*. . . .

Library of Congress Catalog Card Number: 64–22375
Manufactured in the United States of America
First Edition

DANIEL HALÉVY

My Friend Degas

TRANSLATED

AND EDITED WITH NOTES BY

MINA CURTISS

Wesleyan University Press
MIDDLETOWN, CONNECTICUT

My Friend Degas : Contents

My Friend Degas : Illustrations

A Note on the Text

THE CORE of *My Friend Degas* is a translation of *Degas parle
. . .* , published by La Palatine, Paris, 1960. Before the author's
death in February, 1962, he rewrote portions of the text, de-
leted others, and made a number of additions. These changes
made it necessary for the editor to adjust the chronological order. The 1891–1892 portions of M. Halévy's journal and a letter
from Degas, which had been published in the Grasset 1945 edition of *Lettres de Degas,* were also added.

M. Halévy's notes are initialled D.H. All others are by the editor, who has tried to base them as frequently as possible on the
author's autobiographical *Pays Parisiens,* Grasset, Paris, 1932,
on *Lettres de Degas,* and on other contemporary sources.

The illustrations in this book are reproduced from the best
obtainable prints, the negatives being unavailable. They come
from the personal collection of Madame Joxe, M. Halévy's
daughter, and the collection of M. Jean Nepveu-Degas in the
Bibliothèque Nationale. Their generosity in allowing the re-
production of these prints and the cooperation of M. Jean
Adhémar, Curator of the Department of Prints and Engravings
of the Bibliothèque Nationale, are gratefully acknowledged.

My Friend Degas : Preface

My Friend Degas is both Daniel Halévy's earliest book and his last, for he started keeping the journal that forms a large part of it in 1888, when he was sixteen, and was working on revisions of it when he died in 1962 at the age of ninety. That these youthful memoirs should be M. Halévy's first book to be translated into English is ironical since over a period of seventy years he published a dozen or more scholarly works which won him wide recognition in France as a great authority on the intellectual and political life of the Second Empire and the Third Republic.

Scholarship came naturally to M. Halévy by inheritance, environment, and his own wide-ranging intellectual curiosity. His great-grandfather, Elie Halévy, who came to France from Germany in the late eighteenth century, was, in the words of his son Léon, "very well-versed in Talmudic studies and much honored among the Israelites because of his character and learning." Léon himself, Daniel's grandfather, a classical scholar and ardent devotee of the theatre, was in his youth secretary to the philosopher Saint-Simon. He married the daughter of Hippolyte Lebas, permanent secretary of the Académie des Beaux-Arts and official architect of the Institut, where he lived for many years surrounded by generations of his offspring, and where Daniel's father, Ludovic, was born. The latter, co-author with Meilhac of innumerable light comedies, libretti for several works by Offenbach and for Bizet's *Carmen*, author of *La Famille Cardinale*

9

and *L'Abbé Constantin,* became one of the forty "immortals" of the French Academy. His wife, Daniel's mother, was a descendant of Louis Breguet, the master clockmaker who emigrated from Switzerland to Paris in the 1760's and who also became a member of the Institut.

On the advice of Renan, who was a family friend, M. Halévy took his university degree in Arabic studies, yet while still a student he translated Nietzsche's attack on Wagner and later wrote a biography of the German philosopher. Apart from biographies of Michelet, of Proudhon, of President Wilson, of the poet Charles Péguy, he wrote a number of historical studies, among them *La Fin des Notables* and *La République des Ducs.* But he is perhaps best known for his long co-editorship with Péguy of *Les Cahiers de la Quinzaine,* where the early writings of Mauriac, Malraux and Montherlant first appeared.

Because his name is associated with *La Juive,* the opera composed by his great-uncle Fromental Halévy, and because of his pro-Dreyfus stand during the Affair, it is generally assumed that M. Halévy was a Jew. His attitude towards what he called the "diversity" of his religious heritage is perhaps best explained by a letter in which he quotes his father as saying, " 'How could I be anti-Semitic when my father was a Jew? How could I be anti-Catholic when my mother was a Catholic? How could I be anti-Protestant when my wife, my children are Protestants?' This wisdom," M. Halévy continues, "Péguy summarized for me one day: 'You, Halévy, must respect them all.' Let anyone point out a page of my work or an act of my life where I have failed in this triple respect." Although this principle of tolerance gave rise to certain inconsistencies in his political opinions over the years, it was perhaps also responsible for his steadfast loyalty to Degas after the painter's anti-Semitism caused a break in his friendship with the Halévy family over the Dreyfus Affair.

"The reader must not expect a unity of tone," the author wrote early in this book. Nor must he expect it in this preface. M. Halévy was my friend. And as Robert Garric wrote in his obituary notice in the newspaper *Le Monde,*

Everyone who knew him well already feels that he has lost a true friend, a wise and dependable counselor. . . . At ninety he welcomed newcomers, both French and foreign, with the same indulgence and warmth as when he was forty. . . . In recent years this great reader and scholar could no longer see. But he did not surrender. Gently stoical and without ever complaining, he had books and manuscripts read to him; he dictated articles and continued to surround himself with friends who treasure the moving memory of his splendid presence.

It is as one of these foreign friends, who for fifteen years rejoiced in the generous gifts of his mind and heart, that I wish to write about Daniel Halévy.

It was in 1947 when I was working on a translation of some letters of Marcel Proust that I went first to the eighteenth-century house in the Quai de l'Horloge which M. Halévy inherited through the line of his great-grandfather, the clockmaker. The house, although it is classified as a national monument, is not impressive nor conducive to formality. The *concierge* simply told me to go upstairs and knock on the first door to the left. When M. Halévy welcomed me into what I later discovered was his combined study and bedroom I felt that I had indeed walked back into an earlier century. The small, crowded room, with its view of the Seine, contained a couch-bed, a huge desk, an armchair covered in faded amber velvet. Books were scattered everywhere; on the walls hung many drawing by Degas and charming family portraits by Jacques-Emile Blanche. M. Halévy himself, with his full beard, his long hair, his sensitive intellectual face, his bright, inquiring eyes, seemed to me to have stepped out of one of Nadar's sharply defined photographs.

In the forefront of my mind as I climbed the stairs was a letter Proust had written at the age of fifteen to a schoolmate: "Are you trying to tell me that Halévy thinks I am raving mad . . . insufferable, that my eagerness seemed to him — sage that he is — at first ridiculous, and very soon tiresome; that he wanted me to feel that I was too clinging and wished to be rid of me?" Early in our conversation I said to M. Halévy, "You were very severe

11

with Proust, weren't you?" "Worse that that," he replied. "Harsh, even ruthless." Yet, although he was never really quite reconciled to the world-wide fame achieved by his difficult schoolmate, he included in *Pays Parisiens,* the delightful memoir of his youth, an endearing account of his and Marcel's attempt to present a bouquet to a dairy-maid with whom they were both infatuated at the respective ages of fourteen and fifteen.

I first went to see M. Halévy to ask his help in finding the originals of Proust's letters to Madame Straus, a first cousin of Ludovic Halévy and the widow of Georges Bizet. Through the clue M. Halévy gave me I found not only the Proust letters but all of Fromental Halévy's and Bizet's family papers as well. This discovery resulted in my writing a biography of the composer, a project in which M. Halévy gave me the greatest encouragement, although he, a Wagnerian, a passionate pilgrim to Bayreuth even in his eighties, had no taste for Bizet's music nor much interest in him as a man. But he gave me free access to all the Halévy family papers, many of which he himself had never troubled to examine.

The journal which his father kept for over thirty years became the basis of my work each morning for two months in a bitter cold winter when I sat before a window at 39 Quai de l'Horloge in the second floor salon which was heated only by a tiny stove. M. Halévy would come in, sometimes in his dressing-gown, bringing wood to start the fire while I, wrapped in woolen clothing and a fur-lined coat which I never removed, warmed my feet in a small fur hearth-rug which Madame Halévy brought me the first day. Absorbed though I was in this adventure into the past, my hands would eventually get so cold I could no longer copy. Then I would wander around the salon which seemed smaller than it was because of the rows of little chairs that lived there. On the walls were Fragonard and Watteau drawings, on the mantelpiece family miniatures. Out the window the barges chugged up and down the Seine. In spite of the cold and the smoke, which sometimes forced me to open the window wide, I felt that I was indeed in a scholar's paradise.

One morning M. Halévy said to me, "I can't understand why a person as young as you should be so absorbed in the past." (He was at the time reading a book by a friend, Taine's niece, about the destruction of Ouradour, the French Lidice.) "The present is so much more interesting. . . . What, for instance, are you copying out now?"

"A letter from your great-uncle Fromental."

"Well, tell me about him," he said. "What was he like?"

"But surely you've read Sainte-Beuve's essay on him?"

"No. What did he say?"

"Well, he said that your uncle was like a bee who never seemed to have found his way into the right hive. If you sat next to him at dinner he never talked about music but about some special subject that had suddenly enthralled him. If he read a book on military history he would decide that he should have been a general. Or a new book on geology would make him think he should have been a scientist. When people were surprised that he continued to hold his position as stage-director at the Opéra after the success of *La Juive* he said, 'But a man can't write operas all day long.' I don't think he was ever quite reconciled to being a musician."

"*Un raté comme moi!*" was M. Halévy's comment.

No one could have been less ineffectual than M. Halévy. But his insatiable curiosity about everything to do with the humanities and human experience did sometimes lead him into domains far afield from his political and historical writing. (He never achieved a work of the permanent importance and bulk of his brother Elie's *History of England in the 19th Century*.) One example of this breadth of interest verged, I thought, on the eccentric.

It was revealed to me when I arrived for tea one day and found all the little chairs in the salon occupied by an extraordinary-looking group of gentlemen. (Madame Halévy and I were the only women.) At first glance I felt as though I had wandered into one of those large group paintings by Fantin-Latour — *Hommage à Delacroix* perhaps. But the men were almost all elderly or old, and the homage was to the sixth Lord

Derby, author of the works of William Shakespeare in the opinion of the majority of those present.

The guest of honor was Abel LeFranc, aged ninety-two, a tall, handsome man with a long white beard and a splendid head of white hair. In his forties M. LeFranc had been the outstanding world-scholar on Rabelais. But as a result of becoming convinced in middle age of Lord Derby's unrecognized genius, he devoted his remaining half-century to spreading this doctrine. Among the other Derbyites were a small, huffy, very aged and aggressive admiral, a member of the Académie Française, and Professor Cazamian of the Sorbonne, author of *Histoire de la Littérature Anglaise,* who may perhaps have been merely a potential convert.

The meeting opened with a little speech by M. Halévy who wore a high-necked, double-breasted navy blue jacket with a flowing black tie. His beard and long hair had been smartly trimmed for the occasion. His friend Degas would have found him an admirable subject for a portrait. After a brief tribute to M. LeFranc he explained that the meeting had been called because the success of the Comtesse de Chambrun's latest work on Shakespeare had caused the Derbyites to feel that some action was indicated to advance their cause. Methods of propaganda were discussed, the "Stratfordites" being frequently referred to as the enemy. My ignorance of the life of the sixth Lord Derby, combined with the conspiratorial atmosphere, not unlike the meeting of an undergraduate secret society, tended to give me a sense of confused inadequacy. During the interval when Madame Halévy served the only really good tea I ever had in Paris, I approached a rosy-faced young man who had arrived late.

"I suppose you understand all about this," I said.

"On the contrary, Madame. I made an appointment a month ago to ask M. Halévy about Léon Blum. You know he went to school with him. Blum is the subject of my doctoral dissertation."

Wide and unpredictable as were the fields into which M. Halévy's active curiosity led him — I never did find out how or when Lord Derby entered his life — Léon Blum or any distinguished political figure was far more relevant to his basic interest. This fact I once forgot to my considerable embarrassment. When I returned to Paris in the autumn of 1952 M. Halévy, who always omitted preliminaries and small talk, greeted me with, "Tell me about Stevenson." The Stevenson who came first to my mind was Robert Louis. Remembering the French cult for Poe, still active, and more or less incomprehensible to an American, I thought that perhaps some French *littérateur* had recently discovered *Treasure Island* or *A Child's Garden of Verses*.

"It's a long time since I have read any Stevenson," I hazarded.

"*Mais non*, Madame, Adlai Stevenson, the candidate for President. You live too much in the past."

There were certain elements of the past, however, that he thought I neglected. He was shocked when he discovered that I had never seen the Basilique de Saint-Denis. I explained that I had looked it up in the *Guide-bleu* and after discovering how many times it had been demolished and reconstructed I decided it was a landmark I could miss; that although I admired the good intentions of Viollet-le-Duc, their execution more frequently than not seemed to me aesthetically disturbing. "You are too thorough, Madame, too thorough." (This was a comment with which he often teased me. What would he think about the notes for this book?) I must see the monuments of the Kings of France, he said, and he would guide me. It was a highly adventurous expedition.

At this time M. Halévy's eyesight was already very much impaired. He could see straight ahead but not to either side. In the walks which he continued as long as possible, just as Degas had in his old age, he carried the white cane of the blind but he crossed streets as though the traffic-lights were non-existent. We went to Saint-Denis in an open car, and whereas the friend who was driving us found the traffic almost unbearable, M. Halévy was enchanted by everything he saw, pointing out landmarks he remembered from the days when he had spent much time in that *quartier*. It was there that at the turn of the century he and a group of other intellectual young men had started the *Univer-*

sité populaire, an experiment in adult education which greatly influenced his thinking throughout his life. When we arrived at the church he climbed the stairs so fast that I could barely keep up with him. Inside a guide was conducting a group of tourists whom we joined. But M. Halévy, not satisfied with the guide's limited spiel, added his own comments much to the satisfaction of the visitors who proceeded to follow him rather than the guide. In some miraculous way M. Halévy never stumbled over the many levels in the church. But my anxiety that he might fall so dimmed my capacity either to listen or to observe the monuments of the Kings of France that all I remember is a large expanse of grim ugliness. The beauty lay in the wonderful richness of his mind, his interest and enthusiasm at the age of eighty-five, and above all in his superb ignoring of any physical danger.

In *My Friend Degas* M. Halévy tells of a walk he, at forty, took with Degas who was then eighty years old. "I joined him on the sidewalk of the rue de la Ville-l'Evèque and accompanied him. Or rather he accompanied me, walking for the sake of walking as he does these days. . . . He steps up and down the curbstones, crosses the streets pretty well. I was constantly worried about him, but I was wrong. It is impossible to tell how much or how little he sees. He stopped all of a sudden — this was always a habit of his — as if to tell me something important. 'I sleep very well,' he said, 'eight or nine hours a night. I can still sleep and I still have my legs.' . . . His higher faculties are growing numb. . . . Nevertheless he is interested in everything — in the Balkan war, for instance — but from so far away. Always those eighty years. The distance is very long between him and us."

Between M. Halévy in his eighties and us the distance did not seem long. Indeed, not until he was in his ninetieth year could one describe him as he did Degas in 1913: "Degas is still so beautiful. The semi-absence that foretells death; and yet as soon as one speaks to him, such presence, such energy, such clarity of voice and eye." That is how Daniel Halévy was the last time I saw him.

16

Not until M. Halévy was deprived of his eyesight and the ability to move freely, as Degas had been, did he decide to publish *Degas parle* . . . , based on the journal in which he had recorded the words of the great painter who had been his idol. M. Halévy was eager above all that this book should appear in translation in the United States and England, but he was not to live to see his hopes fulfilled. On the day he died I received a letter he had dictated four days earlier, telling me that he had reread his book with great care (it would never have occurred to him to say that it had been read to him), and had added "some meditations that were not in the original volume, which adhered very closely to the childhood source." His secretary, he said, was making a copy to be sent to me as soon as he had finished "reviewing her work." I can only hope that he would not have found the translation and the notes too faulty. In any case, I should like to dedicate them to his memory.

MINA CURTISS

Bethel, Connecticut
April, 1964

My Friend Degas

My Friend Degas : Introduction

Degas's remarks which are given in this book are drawn from a journal that I kept in my youth. The first of these remarks dates from 1888. At that time I was no longer a child, I was sixteen years old — an adolescent. But I knew Degas long before my adolescence. His relationship with my parents was life-long. For my father it started in the courtyard of the old Lycée Louis-le-Grand where they had been schoolmates. At the time of the Second Empire, they met again backstage at the Opéra which was then the center of one of the pleasantest groups in Paris. Degas had illustrated my father's book, *La Famille Cardinale,* and the fine portrait he drew of my father shows him in the foyer of the Opéra. Degas's friendship with my mother was different; to her he was like a member of the family. She had known the Degas, both parents and children. She admired the father, a knowledgeable lover of ancient Italian music and a friend of several of the best musicians of his day. She was an intimate friend of his daughter, Marguerite, and her friendship with Degas was quasi-fraternal. Degas and my parents lived in the same quarter of Paris, a Montmartre then inhabited by writers and artists. Two or three times a week Degas would leave his studio, ring our doorbell and sit down at table with us.

Hence my unique recollection of his character. All Paris knew him as a fighter, a recluse, guarding his privacy with cruel, crushing words. The habitués of the Paris boulevards defended themselves against his scorn by accusing him of insincerity. "Degas," they said, "would like to see his reflection in a boulevard window in order to give himself the satisfaction of breaking the plate-glass with his cane." What nonsense! Even as a child I knew that Degas was a man who suffered. First there was his eyesight. My mother explained to me that his eyes had been injured by the sharp cold of the nights he had spent as sentinel during the Siege of Paris. What was the real nature of this eye-disease? The oculists seem never to have understood it. According to several of Degas's statements, he experienced increasing difficulty in establishing outlines. Innumerable attempts were found after his death. We know that for long hours he rested lying down in his studio in order to regain his energy. I shall not insist on this point which has become common knowledge. Degas is the painter who went blind as Beethoven is the composer who became deaf.

But there is another disaster barely known to the public and too little known even to those who have studied Degas's life. I was aware of it before I was ten years old. This disaster was financial. It ruined one of his brothers and threatened the honor of his name.

The practice of banking was traditional in the Degas family. It had been their business in Paris before the Revolution; and when around 1792 they had been forced to flee revolutionary Paris, the Degas settled in Naples where they opened a bank which became very successful. It was around 1930 that the philosopher Benedetto Croce, a Neapolitan, showed me the house that he still called the Degas house. Degas's father was an ardent art-lover who lived off his income, but one of his sons had again taken up the family calling and worked on the Stock Exchange. The fact is that in 1878 there was a pistol shot in the Bourse in Paris; the man who shot himself was a Degas who had gone bankrupt.

To understand what followed we must remember Degas's intense sensitiveness. He accepted the complete responsibility for which he was in no way obligated. He paid the full amount of the debts. His way of life changed completely. He had been living in the rue Blanche, in a modest but very pleasant house. He disposed of it. He gave up everything he owned and rented a studio at the foot of an alley off the rue Pigalle.

I went there one morning with my father; the new dwelling repelled me and I felt that our friend had been in some way degraded. I asked my mother for an explanation. "When a member of a family," she explained, "owes money and can't pay it, the honor of the family demands that his brothers pay." My mother uttered these words so firmly that I didn't dare repeat the question although the answer left me disturbed. Not until fifteen years later was I able to question a friend who was working in a lawyer's office. My question astonished him. He replied that as far as he knew the practice of which I had spoken was no longer observed. Was it observed in 1880? I suspect that the only basis for that generosity to which I was witness when I was nine years old lay in the indomitable exigencies of Degas's heart. He could not endure a stain on the honor of his family name. His vision of the world darkened. The rather unsociable Degas whose image has persisted dates from that time. I think he had enjoyed receiving his friends in his pleasant house in the rue Blanche; I think the studio in the Cité Pigalle was the first refuge of his anti-social feelings. There he ceased to be an artist wealthy enough to choose his models. He became an impoverished painter who had to earn his living and support his brothers who had become poor like himself. However, he never tried in any way to please the public. His choice of new models was a sign of his depression. Formerly he had been preoccupied by ballet dancers and horses. Henceforth he would choose as models people exhausted by hard work or worn out by the routine of a life of shame.

The naturalist writers had just introduced houses of prostitution into literature. Degas amused himself one evening by making illustrations for the Goncourts' *La Fille Elisa*. Soon he himself went into the houses and made lithographs so brutal that they are still locked up in various portfolios.

This same Degas who had so fervently studied the ballet

dancer in action, now started studying the motions of women dressing, bathing, and twisting their bodies while drying themselves. Later, looking back on his past, he would feel a certain sadness and would write to a friend that he wished he might have lived at the time when his predecessors, unaware of women in bath-tubs, painted Susanna and the Elders.

Although thus cut off from society, Degas did not abandon the Impressionist exhibitions that he himself had started. Indeed, he announced a new exhibition. Only the name was changed to the Exhibition of Independent Painters. Actually the word Impressionist in no way suited Degas who ignored the outdoors and worked passionately between the four walls of his studio. The chief work that he showed was a series of seventeen drawings, an ensemble that impressed all visitors by the authority of their line. Huysmans admired these drawings, all of which show the nude in various intimate attitudes. He noted that there was no effort at grace, that the awkwardness was frequent and deliberate. Huysmans was astonished at the "misogyny." "Misogyny," the word thus applied to the painter for the first time, henceforth became the term that for many people characterized Degas.[1]

1.   This exhibition took place in 1886. Joris-Karl Huysmans, the novelist, practiced art criticism between 1879 and 1888. He was the first critic to recognize Degas's greatness and to do justice to Pissarro and Gauguin. He "discovered" Raffaëlli, Forain, and Odilon Redon. His favorite painter was Gustave Moreau.

The article to which M. Halévy refers appeared in a collection of Huysmans' essays, *Certains,* published in Paris in 1887. The relevant passage follows:

"Review of an exhibition described in the catalogue as 'Series of nudes, women in their baths, washing themselves, drying themselves, wiping themselves while having their hair combed.'

"M. Degas, who in his admirable pictures of ballerinas has already so implacably rendered the awkwardness of the dancer, deformed by the mechanical monotony of her professional leaps and bounds, has this time brought to his studies of nudes a careful cruelty, a patient hate.

"It seems as though, exasperated by the sordidness of his surroundings, he must have wished to make reprisals, to hurl the most

I MUST NOW speak of a totally different Degas and tell of a feeling shared by all men, but not equally. I shall write the word "mourning," which according to my dictionary means: "Affliction caused by the death of a beloved person." Degas's extreme sensibility in this realm ceases to be surprising if we know the bitter fact that he lost his mother when he was seventeen. From then on his father lived a solitary life. A few friends were admitted, mostly musicians like Pagans, famous for his playing of ancient Italian music. Degas *père* spent many long hours listening to this music. This brief picture sums up memories that colored Degas's youth and left their mark on his whole life.

At the time of which I am speaking one of Degas's friends suffered a great sorrow. The painter Bartholomé[2] lost his young wife. Would he survive so cruel a blow? This question must be taken in the full force of its meaning. Degas, himself so deeply imbued with sorrow, became the almost inseparable companion of Bartholomé, now a man of sorrows himself.

---

flagrant insult at his century by demolishing its most constantly enshrined idol, woman, whom he debases by showing her in her tub, in the humiliating positions of her intimate ablutions. . . .

"But in addition to this special accent of scorn and hate, what we must see in these works is the unforgettable veracity in the drawing, so intrinsically rich in its lucid and controlled ardor, its icy fever. What we must see is the intense yet muffled coloring, the mysterious and opulent tone of these scenes. . . .

"A powerful and isolated artist, with no established precedents, with no followers that matter, M. Degas arouses in each of his pictures the sensation of a calculated strangeness, of such exact insight that we are surprised, and almost blame ourselves for being astonished. His realism is of the kind that that brute Courbet could never achieve, but which certain Primitives imagined; that is to say an art expressing an exuberant urge in live bodies, cut off from the soul, but in perfect accord with their surroundings."

2. Paul Bartholomé (1848–1928) was a painter until 1887 when he gave up painting for sculpture. His best known work is the *Monument aux Morts* in the Père Lachaise cemetery.

As a child I knew about this. Degas told us of his friend's suffering. Bartholomé, he told us, wanted to become a sculptor in order to carve a monument for his wife's grave so that his art, that is to say his work, would be inseparable from his grief. Degas described to us the monument that Bartholomé wanted to raise on his wife's grave: *Jesus dying on the cross,* his head bent, his mouth open in a final cry of despair. Lemoisne, in his splendid life of Degas, adds a fact that as a child I didn't know. He says that it was Degas's idea that Bartholomé should become a sculptor. For Degas, indefatigable experimenter that he was, had learned the technique of sculpture and thought it a more suitable medium to express profound suffering. From the first to the last day Degas followed the conception, the work of his friend.

Bartholomé, not without great effort, succeeded in producing his statue and Degas told us of the joy he felt when he saw Bartholomé's *Christ* erected in the cemetery at Crépy-en-Valois. The day the statue was erected I heard him defend Bartholomé's work against the criticism of several other artists.

There is no doubt but what throughout his life the tragedy of bereavement deeply moved Degas. The remarkable thing is that this emotion never lessened. When he was very old I saw Degas travel across the whole of France to attend the funeral of an old friend. He was not at all given to metaphysical speculation, but grief expanded his mind and his emotions attained a higher level. I remember leaving a church with him one day after a mass for the dead. Degas lifted his head, and looking at the high nave he murmured, "That Catholic liturgy, that great wheel that turns." The death of someone he loved shook him in his whole being.

FAMILY PROBLEMS distressed him profoundly, too. The day he came to tell us about one there was a stranger at our table. Degas remained silent about anything personal but about every other subject he exploded with such violence that my parents were embarrassed. Finally the stranger left. Alone with us Degas said,

"My sister Marguerite has just left for the Argentine with her husband and her children. Her husband lost a great deal of money speculating on real estate. I am just back from Le Havre. I saw them off. If I hadn't been there she couldn't even have taken all her luggage. . . ."

Marguerite, his beloved sister, my mother's friend. Art-lovers know her through Degas's beautiful drawing that shows her standing, holding a sheet of music in her hand, her lips open in song. Degas was never to see her again; of this grief few were aware. But in Degas's life it was the beginning of a fresh sense of desolation.

As I HAVE SAID, the subject-matter of this book will be largely the remarks and the replies of every kind that I heard from the lips of Degas during my adolescence. However, before I start quoting from my notebooks I shall recall an incident that dates from a time before I was old enough to take notes.

It seems that at table my parents reported to Degas some impertinent remark I had made, and this elicited from him a reply that might well have been spoken at the Montmartre café, the *Rat Mort:* "He is vicious; he will go far." Immediately my mother said, "How can you, Degas, say such a thing in front of this child?" Whereupon Degas answered very gently, "You are right, Louise. I shouldn't have said it."

Degas had been scolded, scolded because of me. This I never forgot.

My Friend Degas : Chapter I

SEVERAL SUMMERS between 1882 and 1887 my parents took my brother and me to Dieppe on vacation. Our friends, the Blanche family, had built onto their villa a fine studio for their painter son, Jacques-Emile Blanche. This villa at the extreme western end of the beach stood alone between the high cliff and the sea. Four other villas stood in a row near theirs and the closest of these my parents rented. It was large enough so that they could have as guests their two most intimate friends, Degas and Cavé.[1]

In my journal for 1887 I find some of Degas's charming re-

1. "Cavé's eminence lay in the fact that he did nothing all his life.
. . . I often hear talk of people who do nothing, but if I examine their lives, if I think of the way our friend Cavé led his, it always seems to me that these people are false idlers; that their leisure stems from wealth, boredom or laziness, never from a vocation or a genius for it.
. . . How many men know how to be idle? One man develops a passion for breeding greyhounds, another solemnly administers his fortune, another makes a serious cult of some secret vice. But Cavé belonged in no category; he ignored his holdings; he neither kept animals nor indulged in vices.

"His delightful witty remarks charmed many who repeated or appropriated them. . . . His invisible wit spangled many of the light comedies written during the Second Empire. Cavé's mere presence, his advice were of the greatest value during rehearsals. 'What does Cavé have to say?' Dumas would ask. Everybody asked, 'What does Cavé say?' He was exempt from that sort of tension, of inflexibility which is the occupational deformation of the professional. Always interested, always available . . . he embodied the audience in its pure and

marks about Cavé: "Cavé, that compound of leisure and taste," and "Cavé is so indifferent that he slides any question into his lap like a man drawing a shawl over his knees to protect himself from the cold."

The academician, John Lemoinne,[2] a close friend of the Blanches, came each year to Dieppe with his three daughters, the oldest of whom, Rose, married Jacques-Emile at the turn of the century. We were all very intimate during our stay at Dieppe, and Degas found a nickname for the three young girls. He called them *"les petites amies."*

Our social life was enlivened by a variety of friends who came and went: young Paul Helleu[3] and Walter Sickert.[4] One

perfect form: the public of one's dreams, one's ideals, one's wishful thinking. . . .

"I like to think of that bizarre couple among our friends, Degas and Cavé: Degas, toil incarnate, Cavé, the enemy of toil. Degas had long regarded him with astonishment. What sort of man was this? But Cavé had so much taste that one couldn't help appreciating him. 'That Cavé,' Degas would say, to explain, to justify his indulgence, 'that Cavé is so gracious.' It amused him to imitate the gestures Cavé made with his arms when he talked. 'That Cavé,' he would say, 'that Cavé is a ballet-dancer . . .'" Daniel Halévy, *Pays Parisiens,* Paris, 1932.

2. John Lemoinne (1815–1892) was for many years editor of the *Journal des Debats.* He became a Senator and was a member of the Académie Française.

3. Paul Helleu (1859–1927) in the eighteen-eighties was at the beginning of his brilliantly successful career as a fashionable etcher and painter in pastel. Launched under the patronage of Comte Robert de Montesquiou he was introduced into the highest society where his etchings, drawings, and pastel portraits of rich and beautiful women became highly prized. He did six portraits of the then Duchess of Marlborough (*née* Vanderbilt).

A passionate admirer of Degas, he deplored the fact that the master did not paint pretty women. At a time when Helleu was enamored of Watteau, Degas was said to have described him as a "Watteau *à vapeur,*" a play of words on *bateau à vapeur* or steamboat. Many years later Degas denied authorship of this damaging but not inaccurate description.

4. Walter Richard Sickert (1860–1942) was first a disciple of Whistler and then of Degas, both of whose influences seem to be be-

30

summer even Whistler came and gave an informal lecture at his friends, the Gobdens', which Mallarmé translated.[5] Our days were spent in long walks with pauses for rest at nearby farmhouses. Sometimes conversation would lag and at our request Degas would tell us Oriental tales. He was very fond of them, and his extraordinary memory enabled him to recall entire stories from the *Arabian Nights*. But our rest-periods were not as long as Schéherézade's nights, and Degas satisfied us with less. After more than seventy years I can still tell two of the stories — the one about the borrowed pots and the bad friend, and the one about the young fakir.

Now I shall quote from the notes I made between 1888 and 1897. An adolescent of sixteen will take over. The reader must not expect a unity of tone in this book.

---

lied in a statement of his quoted by Virginia Woolf in her *Walter Sickert: A Conversation,* London, 1934: "I have always been a literary painter, thank goodness, like all the decent painters." Mrs. Woolf continues, "Among the many kinds of artists, it may be that there are some who are hybrid. . . . Sickert it may be is among the hybrids, the raiders. . . . I have read that he is part German, part English, part Scandinavian perhaps; he was born in Munich, was educated at Reading, and lived in France. . . . He is probably the best painter now living in England."

When in 1934 Walter Richard Sickert was elected to membership in the Royal Academy, of which he had been an associate since 1924, he dropped his first Christian name and became Richard Sickert. A year later when he resigned from the academy he reverted to Walter.

5.   In September, 1885, Degas commented on this lecture to Ludovic Halévy: ". . . What's this I hear? That you are going to analyze in Hébrard's column in *Le Temps* the lecture that Louise [Mme Halévy] translated? If you treat it seriously, I shall laugh at you like a member of the Academy. If it's the *Ten O'Clock,* there you have irony, there you have art scorned by society in evening dress, there you have *le bonheur.* Whistler will leave the choice between the two approaches to you. But what he himself wants is quite simple. He wants you to talk about him according to his own lights." *Lettres de Degas,* Paris, 1945.

At one point, Degas, exacerbated by Whistler's vanity, said to him, "My dear Whistler, you behave like a man without talent."

31

26 October 1888

Monsieur Degas has just lunched here. And Degas lunches are for me the greatest feasts imaginable. In my eyes Degas is the incarnation of all intelligence.

Today he defined education as follows: "It consists in making a man unfit for any number of occupations by which he might earn his living. In the past ballerinas were the daughters of *concierges;* now they are given diplomas by the government!"

And later he said, "I now see that it is only late in life that a man can read. When you are young your aim is to finish the book. When you are old you want to slow down. Re-reading a book for the second or third time you are struck by the details. Every line has a fresh meaning." And he ended by saying, "You must have five favorite books and never abandon them."

28 October 1888

This summer Sickert came to see Mama. He talked about Degas in a way that was a revelation to me. He expressed in one word, purity, the life of this man — it would have been so easy, he said, for Degas, with his intransigence, to have made his name notorious. Never anything of the kind. And with this remark Degas appeared to me as one of the ancient giants of righteousness: those whose virtue is legendary. But Degas is not yet a legend!

12 November 1888

Monsieur Degas said today: "There are some women who should barely be spoken to; they should only be caressed." . . .

27 May 1889

Tonight at dinner Reyer,[6] Degas, Cavé — witty. The talk was of law-suits.

6. Ernest Reyer (1828–1909), composer of the operas *La Statue, Erostrate,* and *Sigurd,* a close friend and disciple of Berlioz, succeeded his master as music critic on the *Journal des Débats.* He and Degas, who were friends of long standing, shared a number of characteristics.

Degas as a young man.
Photograph attributed to Nadar.
Courtesy of Bibliothèque Nationale.

Degas in his studio.
Posed by himself, photographed by Bartholomé.
Courtesy of Bibliothèque Nationale.

"Halévy," Degas said, "you should have been a lawyer."

"I did study law for a while," my father[7] replied. "It bored me to death."

"I did, too," said Degas. "While I was doing it I copied all

Reyer, considered by the general public a rude, crotchety, disgruntled man, was regarded by his friends as affectionate, helpful, and generous. His wit, like Degas's was very personal. On the occasion of a festival in honor of Berlioz after the great composer's death a man came up to Reyer and asked him for a ticket. "I haven't any," Reyer said. "If Berlioz were alive," the man protested, "I should have a seat in the first row." "If Berlioz were alive," Reyer replied, "there wouldn't be any festival."

In *Croquis de Degas,* Ed. Daniel Halévy, Paris, n.d., there is a delightful caricature of Reyer sitting in an opera box surrounded by three of the painter's typical laundresses.

7. Ludovic Halévy (1834–1908), a Parisian born and bred for whom his birthplace never lost its enchantment, knew success early. As secretary at the age of twenty-nine to the powerful Duc de Morny, half-brother of Napoleon III and president of the *Corps Legislatif,* he could himself have acquired great power and wealth. But after the death of his patron he wrote in his journal, "Of my own free will I renounced the future opportunities offered by my position at the *Corps Legislatif.* With no difficulty at all I devoted myself eagerly to my work in the theatre and quickly achieved security and independence in my life. If I died tomorrow I should leave some fifty thousand francs. . . . To give my family a happier and broader life is my ambition. For myself I wish for nothing."

Whatever his wishes, fortune and his gifts favored him. So successful were he and Meilhac in the forty or more comedies and farces they wrote together and the libretti for a number of Offenbach's operas that the general public, according to one critic, pictured them as privileged creatures who used the laps of duchesses for desks, writing only with pens taken from the brilliant plumage of rare Asiatic birds.

The best-known work for which Halévy and Meilhac supplied a libretto was Bizet's *Carmen* which when first produced in 1875 was a failure. Thereafter Halévy wrote little for the theatre but published several works of fiction, including *L'Abbé Constantin* and *La Famille Cardinale.* The latter consisted of sketches based on conversations with ballet dancers and their parents backstage at the Opéra.

A passionate archivist, Ludovic Halévy kept a journal which is in itself a rich history of political and social France of the period.

The Dreyfus Affair left him very much changed, subject to spells of amnesia and melancholia. He died in 1908.

33

the primitives at the Louvre. I ended by telling my father that I couldn't go on."

"What did he say?"

"Nothing at all."

"A good father. Wasn't that when you moved to a small apartment of your own?"

"No, not until later."

"Why don't you tell us something about your youth? You never talk about it."

Degas was silent and looked at the ceiling; he seemed sad. His youth had not been happy. Degas's father adored painting. He was a very gentle, very distinguished, very kind man, witty, and above all devoted to music and painting. His daughters sang Gluck choruses for him and at night he shut himself in his salon and improvised softly on the piano. The father did not like what his son painted and, as Degas thought highly of his father's taste, he was disturbed by his disapproval. This never caused any coolness between them, but it made their relationship difficult. The father did not even want to see his son's work. But one day he came back from a visit to the Salon. "I saw a really remarkable painting," he said to his son, "a portrait hung very high in such-and-such a room. I couldn't see the artist's name. Do you know?"

It was by Degas. What joy for him!

Degas! What a man! Some of his paintings were hung in the Centenary exhibition. He had them removed after violent scenes with Antonin Proust,[8] and in spite of the committee's decision to ignore his order. Perhaps this behavior was slightly exaggerated, but exaggeration is almost inseparable from a will-power as firm as Degas's, and an equally intense hatred of publicity.

8. Antonin Proust (1832–1905) studied painting in Couture's studio at the same time as Manet who painted several portraits of him. He gave up painting for journalism and became an early follower of Gambetta, under whom he served as Minister of Fine Arts for a few months in 1881. He was five times elected a Republican deputy and was the author of *l'Art sous la République* (1891) and *Edouard Manet* (1897).

34

6 October 1889

"I want to write an article about Degas," George Moore[9] told us. "But I wanted to do it once before and we nearly quarreled over it. What do you think about it? You know the exaggerated tone that I'll take . . . exaggerated! What I mean to say is . . ."

That "exaggerated" was funny.

28 October 1889

At Marnes we lived in a charming, old house. On the street side there was a sanded courtyard and in back a rather large garden. This garden, close to the house, was planned like the gardens of all suburban villas. Fortunately it could be transformed into a vast French vegetable garden, spread out in neat rows, with strawberry beds and onions, bordered by a thick box-hedge. And way at the end was the summer-house, a little building with only one room. It had an antique pediment supported by two columns; and by the door there was a heavy balustrade all covered with wisteria and other vines. Here Degas said to us one day, "I have just read this adorable sentence in the memoirs of an old captain of the time of the Empire: 'I went last night to Madame T——'s ball. Two young people who were dancing in the foyer opened the door for me.' "

9. George Moore (1852–1933), the Anglo-Irish writer, first went to Paris in 1873 to study painting under the academician Alexandre Cabanel. After two or three years of contempt for the Impressionists, he became infatuated with them and with Manet and Degas, about whom he wrote repeatedly, often inaccurately, but with great enthusiasm. Théodore Duret, friend and historian of the Impressionists, wrote of Moore in the seventies, "I was one of Moore's first friends in Paris. . . . I remember him as a golden-haired fop, an aesthete before the days of Wilde. He came to Paris to study painting but soon fell under the influence of the Naturalists and turned to writing. None of us thought anything of him as a writer, but he was very welcome wherever he went, for his manners were amusing and his French very funny." Joseph Hone, *The Life of George Moore,* New York, 1936.

Last night I had a success. Degas and Cavé were dining with us. I quoted a very curious article by Jacques Saint-Cère about Emin and Stanley.[1] Degas immediately said, "I don't suppose you have reached your age without acquiring a certain scorn for the *Figaro?*"

Then he started teasing me. I replied with a remark so little out of the ordinary that I shan't even write it down; it would spoil my triumph. (At the same time it is true that tone of voice and quickness are the essence of repartee.)

"Very good, very good, Daniel," Cavé said, laughing. "Very good indeed! That will teach you to pick your words, Degas."

(Degas, in fact, habitually hurls remarks at people and teases them without anyone's daring to reply.)

"What are these young people coming to?" Degas said with a smile.

6 June 1890

. . . I was turning the leaves of a book and didn't hear very well what they were talking about. "He loved! He lived!" I heard Jacques Blanche exclaim from time to time. That happy man was Berlioz. "Berlioz!" he cried, right in the middle of a beautiful passage I was reading. "Long live Degas and Berlioz! Long live the soft-hearted!" I was turning the pages of my book and seemed to hear Mama declare that Degas was anything but soft-hearted while Jacques pinned her down with well-constructed sentences flaunting such expressions as "obtuse misjudgments" and "false conceptions of life."

. . . Jacques also said that nothing seemed to him as precious as the friendship of a man as marvelous as Degas. He has lunched with us often lately and one day with George Moore. Good old Moore becomes silent the instant Degas appears and watches him with the eyes of a child.

1.   The explorer, Sir Henry Stanley, conducted an expedition to relieve Emin Pasha, governor of the Equatorial Province of Egypt, who had been isolated by the Mahdist rising of 1881–1885.

Mama said to Degas in speaking of his new apartment, "It's charming, but do remove your dressing-room from your picture-gallery. It spoils the whole thing." Degas replied firmly, "No, Louise. It is convenient to me where it is; and I don't put on airs, do I? In the morning I bathe; and then I go back to bed in my nine franc fifty flowered dressing-gown. I am perfectly happy and I say to myself: This is the life of a worker." "But," Mama persisted, "your dressing-room is so funny."

"No, no, Louise! No airs, nothing forced. For a poor man I am well off. Let me stay that way."

Moore said to him: "You revolutionary painters..."

"Revolutionary! Don't say that," said Degas. "We are *tradition* itself. It can't be said too often. And perhaps Titian will say a few words to me as he steps into his gondola."

In speaking of Elie Delaunay's theatrical portrait of Madame Straus[2] as Bizet's widow, Degas also said, "It's studio mourning. She is weeping onto the dado."

1 August 1890

We had Degas for dinner tonight. And since he is practically blind I read aloud to him various pages on art that I found in a collection of French writings. He did not like this remark of Aristotle's: *Nature does not make itself felt in art.* This one he did like: *In the fine arts to reflect is to feel.* Pascal's *What vanity there is in painting* seemed to him specious and false. "That vanity is the grandeur of art," he said. He savored La Bruyère's perfectionism.

We introduced him to a little selection of aphorisms:

Aristotle: *Poetry is truer than History.*

Plato: *Poets and Musicians! Let us crown them with laurel and kick them out.*

Thucydides: *In peacetime sons bury their fathers. In wartime fathers bury their sons.*

We also read him some poems by Victor Hugo. It is a joy to read to this man who daren't read himself at the risk of being

2.   This portrait is now in the Louvre. D.H.

unable to paint; his relative ignorance is part of his greatness. He has read little but knows by heart what he has read. His intellect has developed of its own accord.

[The following letter was written while Degas and Bartholomé were traveling through Burgundy in the autumn of 1890 in a "Tilbury" drawn by a white horse. Ed.]

Degas to Ludovic Halévy

Montereau
1 October 90
Wednesday, 12.30

Everything goes according to schedule. He [the white horse] appeared this morning at six-thirty, not too lively. He started off feebly. There was nothing wrong. Just too much sleep. In the woods near Valence we met some charabancs (in one of them a nice old man was sitting in a red-upholstered Louis XV armchair) full of people in black who must have been coming from a funeral as they looked very happy. He [the horse], pacer that he is, smelled Montereau more than a mile away. The real Hotel Grand Monarque is here, and a real lunch. But I must tell you that the lamb's feet are such as to lure you away from *tête de veau*. Everywhere there are eulogies for the horse, particularly in stables. They guarantee his survival from hour to hour. "Have you had him a long time?" the stableboy asked Bartholomé. "He was born on my place," was the reply. Alas, he has been ours only two days. What might we not have done had we had him in the prime of our lives!

[*Lettres de Degas*]

14 December 1890

Wonderful stories Degas told us this morning — the last two lines of a song in which Cabanel[3] says:

3. Alexandre Cabanel (1823–1889), the ultimately successful academic painter, won all possible honors with his *Birth of Venus*

Moi, je trouve à Michel
Ange un talent réel!

The following episode happened to Cabanel. From his studio he could see everything that happened in a little apartment occupied by two ladies, one young, one old. Every day he watched them, kept track of them. One day they beckoned to him to come downstairs. "Monsieur," said the old lady, the mother, "we feel that we must tell you that from our apartment we can see everything that happens in yours, and as soon as you go out your servant brushes his teeth with your toothbrush."

Another story: Rothschild, at Ferrières. He had two monkeys, two large monkeys, which were particularly carefully watched over by the servants. The night of a reception for the Emperor (Napoleon III) the whole Rothschild family is assembled; and Alphonse de Rothschild, strolling in the park with Lami,[4] is congratulating himself on the splendid occasion. A servant suddenly appears, frantic. The monkeys have escaped into the château. A search has been made; they can't be found.

"I will solve the problem," says Lami. "Call a meeting of the whole family. How many are there?"

"Seventeen," replies Alphonse.

Lami counts the gathering. Instead of seventeen, he finds nineteen persons present. "The two monkeys are here," says he.

"Yes," replies Alphonse, "but how can we recognize them?"

"I will solve the problem," says Lami. And he circulates around the salon asking each person for two louis. Only two give them to him: they are the monkeys.

---

which was bought by Napoleon III. "I do not like this man," wrote Edmond de Goncourt, "with his little crimped grey mustache that looks like an old cat's whiskers. There is something treacherous about his face and his almost dandified elegance clashes with his painter's arty get-up. He is both common and pretentious." *Goncourt Journal*, Vol. XI, Monaco, 1956.

4. Eugène Lami (1800–1890) is best known for his charming watercolors of interiors, showing social life at court and in society.

After dinner Elie[5] and I cornered Degas. He was charming. "I wish there was a decent place in Paris with good music where you could smoke and drink," he said. "In England there is a café, a tavern where they sing Handel choruses."

"But that's foolish," I said. "In Paris you won't find two hundred people who like smoking and drinking with good music."

"You don't know what you're talking about. Paris has everything, even Buddhists.[6] If tomorrow you opened your own little private chapel, you would see men with their wives and children crowding the tramcars to come to it."

"Nevertheless," I said, "I believe that it is wrong to want to hear Gluck or any dramatic music given as an oratorio without scenery and costumes. You yourself told us last summer that after hearing the flute air from *Orpheus* played outdoors against a beautiful landscape you felt as though the music had been left behind in the theatre."[7]

"You didn't understand me," he said. "I thought that music

5.   Elie Halévy (1870–1937), older brother of Daniel, became a professor at the Ecole libre des sciences politiques. He was the author of *La Théorie platonicienne des sciences, La Formation du radicalisme philosophique,* and *Histoire du peuple anglais au XIX⁰ siècle.*

When Ludovic Halévy introduced Elie to the English writer Wilfred Scawen Blunt, in London in the fall of 1895, he noted in his diary that the son, "a most interesting young man of the serious kind one reads of in French novels but so seldom meets, was here on Friday, an abler man, I should say, even than his father."

6.   "My brother informs me that tomorrow morning at the Guimet Museum there is to be a Buddhist mass conducted by two Buddhist priests. If I can't go (I expect my surgeon at the house), you must. You know people in this church. They will invoke the little Goddess who dances. Don't miss this both for your sake and for mine. Details tomorrow evening." Undated pneumatic-telegram from Degas to Bartholomé postmarked 11 P.M. *Lettres de Degas.*

7.   In a letter to Bartholomé, August 28, 1890, from Cauterets where Degas was taking a cure, he wrote, "Yesterday the musicale in the lovely place that I selected. The question is whether I would have found this poignant air more touching if the flute had been accompanied. The answer is no. That flute would have moved me had it been

was one thing and nature another; that art requires its own suitable background."... The conversation turned to reading.

"I can no longer read," he said. "My maid reads me the paper."

I think it was à propos of Zola that we started talking about books.

Degas: "I have read *L'Assommoir, Nana*..."

Me: "You have read *L'Oeuvre,* haven't you?"[8]

Degas: "No."

Me: "But it was at that period that you knew Zola well, wasn't it, that you used to discuss things with him?"

Degas: "No." (His face lighted up.) "It was before that, with Manet and Moore at the *Nouvelle Athènes.* We discussed things endlessly." (He was silent for a moment before continuing.) "Zola's idea of art, cramming everything about a subject into a book, then going on to another subject, seemed to me puerile."

Elie: "It is the idea itself that Zola develops in his art."

Degas was silent for a moment. "Perhaps you are right," he said. "We painters are not synthetically minded. Except in one way perhaps. In a single brush-stroke we can say more than a writer in a whole volume. That is why I flee from these phrase-making critics and all the painters who let themselves be taken in by their edicts. We painters exchange a slang word or two — and that's enough. But we have no general ideas."

Degas then said that he had read Proudhon's book on the arts. I had already heard him speak of Proudhon with a certain admiration.[9]

---

played against a painted backdrop far away from nature. For the presence of nature is insipid in relation to such a work of art and could the idea of happiness move me to tears, it would be when I was unhappy and at the theatre." *Lettres de Degas.*

8. Zola's novel, *L'Oeuvre,* is a study of the lives of young painters, his contemporaries. Critics of the book agreed that the principal character was based on Cézanne. D.H.

9. Daniel Halévy was the author of *La Jeunesse de Proudhon,* Paris, 1913; *La Vie de Proudhon,* Paris, 1948; and *Le Mariage de Proudhon,* Paris, 1955.

Me: "But you seem to know Proudhon well. Haven't I heard you mention him before?"

"Indeed you have," he said. "I have read his *Justice, Art,* and *Confessions.* What admirable books!"

"And he must have been even a better talker than writer."

"Yes. To make a book he took a subject he had developed in conversation and then wrote three hundred pages. It seems that he said little himself but prodded the minds of his companions until an idea turned up. Then he left."

"Have you read his letters? You see him at his best there."

"A few of them."

"Did you ever see him?"

"Once, on the Quai Malaquais. He was wearing a long over-coat with a pleat in the back."

"And he had a head a little like a billy-goat, didn't he?" Elie asked.

"No. A head like Socrates; and he looked at you from behind the glasses he always wore. I remember Madier de Montjau[1] telling how in 1848 when Proudhon was annoyed at Piat he pummeled him, and their friends decided that they must fight a duel. The duel took place, there were some scratches, and that evening Madier saw Proudhon, profoundly humiliated, injured in his dignity as a philosopher by having been willing to kill or be killed for such a petty matter. He was an astonishingly strong man. The strange thing is that he never attacked Veuillot,[2] and that Veuillot never attacked him. They were afraid of each other."

Degas also spoke of the passages in *Justice* on Proudhon's

1. Madier de Montjau (1787–1865), elected deputy in 1830, was loyal to Louis-Philippe until 1841 when he founded a newspaper, *L'Esprit public,* which attacked the government. After the revolution of 1848 he became a legitimist.

2. Louis Veuillot (1813–1883), self-educated journalist and author, after spending Holy Week in Rome in 1837, became an ardent champion of Catholicism. His violent attacks on the moderate Catholics and the Second Empire provoked many duels. He was even imprisoned for his polemics against the University of Paris.

childhood and on literature. He mentioned, too, a note in *Principes de l'Art* on pretty women.

Mallarmé[3] ran into Degas the other day and said to him, "I

3. Mallarmé had been Daniel Halévy's professor of English at the Lycée Condorcet. In *Pays Parisiens,* he wrote of him, "At that time Stéphane Mallarmé was known to only a few artists, but through Degas and Jacques-Emile Blanche I knew that an aura of fitful glory and magic hovered over my professor. This information would have made no impression on me had Mallarmé not really been a magical creature. . . . I can conjure up as though it were only yesterday the living Mallarmé, walking down a school-corridor, greeting a colleague, holding the hand of a child who stumbled against his legs. Although he was rather short and quite simple (just like a French workman, wrote George Moore in *Memoirs of My Dead Life*), his whole appearance embodied an air of great solitude, of secret majesty. He came from his little apartment in the rue de Rome where he had perhaps left the young Claudel or the young Valéry; he crossed the Pont de l'Europe, overcome almost every day, he confided to George Moore, by the desire to jump from the top of the bridge on to the railroad tracks, under the wheels of a train, to escape from the mediocrity that held him prisoner. But he crossed the bridge and came to teach our class.

"He conducted it with exquisite gentleness. We would sit down on our benches and he, climbing the steps of his little platform with his even, rather weary gait, would seat himself at the table which for anyone else I would call professorial. He looked at us, we looked at him, and between us and him we felt an immeasurable distance which did not, however, exclude a remote fraternization. He would indeed have liked to be elsewhere. So would we, and that is perhaps what we sensed. Our other professors exercised a distinct, dominant control over us. . . . With Mallarmé it was entirely different. . . . In the first place no roll-call, no declared presence. Mallarmé was there in his chair, and there we were, our benches facing him. We had the feeling that he came to class like ourselves, with neither great interest nor great resistance, but urged on by an ineluctable force which left him as little focussed, as extraneous as ourselves. The hour went by while he explained rules, dictated in a low musical voice the short (with him always short) exercises, and he, like us, obstinately pursued some revery, not, perhaps, unlike our own.

"I can give an example of the exercises he gave us, having recently found among some old papers a page in my most childish handwrit-

have invented a new word — *damard* — with a 'd' on the end. There was *femmiste,* but I have discovered *damard*. It is to use for an inscription in a book for Hadamard:

> *Quoique n'étant ni femmiste ni damard,*
> *J'en tiens pourtant assez pour Hadamard."*[4]

---

ing, written for this very class. It is dated October 8, 1882 when I was a pupil of his. First an exercise, four lines of English verse:

> I saw a ship a-sailing
> A-sailing on the sea;
> And it was deeply laden
> With pretty things for thee.

Then the translation; here is mine:

> *Je vis un vaisseau naviguer,*
> *Naviguer sur la mer;*
> *Et il était profondément chargé*
> *De jolies choses pour toi.*

After that there was a little theme that Mallarmé made up of the words we had learned in the exercise. Here is the text, which seems to me charming:

— What a fine ship.
— I don't see it.
— A ship sailing on the sea.
— Do you think, mama, it is all filled with pretty things for me, especially candies?
— Perhaps.
— I have not yet seen it.
— Close your eyes and listen to me sing. Then you will see it with everything it contains.

"Am I wrong in thinking that there is poetry in this, a hint of lyricism, and that this childish theme is a little prose poem worthy of being added to Mallarmé's unpublished works? That is the reason, I think, that we were happy to work with him. It takes so little to seduce children and that little is given so grudgingly. . . .

"One day when I was a little late for class I had to pass in front of him to reach my seat. He had thrown a lap-robe over his crossed legs and one of his feet formed a very pronounced point under the cover. To me this point seemed picturesque, like a peak dominating a mountain range, and I indulged in the opportune temptation to hang my hat on this peak. Mallarmé, alerted by the sudden uproar of my

30 December 1890

At dinner Grandmother, my aunt Valentine, and Degas. We have made him not just an intimate friend but a member of our family, his own being scattered all over the world. This makes me very happy. At table we talked about actors and Degas told us this charming story.

"Audry was ill, nervous, sad. He went to consult a doctor. The doctor palpated him, sounded him, examined him thoroughly and said, 'But there is nothing wrong with you. It is just your nerves. You need diversion. Sometimes I get into your state of mind. Then I go out; I go to the Palais-Royal; I go to see Audry.'

---

fellow-pupils, leaned over a little to consider the unusual sight, smiled at first, then with a slight kick tumbled my hat onto the floor. I picked it up at once and hung it on the other hat-rack, the official one. Not a word was spoken and the class began, if indeed the expression 'class' can describe the hour of semi-leisure which was offered us. We occupied our time in talking, sometimes with Mallarmé, more often with each other; and sometimes we drew or exchanged notes. One day (he must have been in a severe mood) he asked me to give him a letter that I was writing. I obeyed reluctantly, for the letter was certainly not meant for him. As chieftain I was addressing to the chief of an enemy band a peace proposal in a Napoleonic style, patterned after one I had just read with great admiration in one of my books. 'Sire,' I wrote, 'For too long have our people suffered the miseries of war. . . .' Mallarmé read, and I, not exactly worried but annoyed by my indiscretion, waited for the end of this sorry business. It was merely disagreeable. Actually, when Mallarmé had finished reading my letter he took up his pen, wrote a few words on the margin and handed it back to me. Then it was my turn to read this humiliating couplet written in red ink

Le petit Daniel
Est un petit sot.

It is embarrassing that these lines should be the clearest of all his work."

4. *Femmiste* exists neither in *Littré* nor *le Grand Larousse*. Roughly translated the inscription reads, "Although I am neither a womanizer nor a lady-killer, I nevertheless approve of it for Hadamard."

" 'I can't do that, doctor. I am Audry.' "

Degas talked about Lourdes which he had recently passed through. My grandmother interrupted him in a critical tone of voice.

"Lourdes," she said, "can you enjoy the spectacle at Lourdes?"

"Bah," Degas replied. "I saw all kinds of people, all kinds of things. A tall young man dressed like a stretcher-bearer, waiting, extremely bored, for some invalid to hire him. I imagine that he had promised to work for a fortnight to please some old aunt who was leaving him something in her will. And then, too, I saw women kneeling, their faces transfigured by faith. I saw lots of things at Lourdes."

But my grandmother insisted, "If someone said that you had lost your mind you know you wouldn't like it!"

"If someone said I had lost my mind," Degas replied, "don't you think I'd be pleased? What use is my mind? Granted that it enables me to hail a bus and pay my fare. But once I am inside my studio, what use is my mind? I have my model, my pencil, my paper, my paints. My mind doesn't interest me."

Discouraged, grandmother was reduced to silence.

9 January 1891

Lots of Degas these days. He came to lunch Wednesday; and à propos of Madame Howland,[5] who still has *shoulders,* he

5. "Nothing about Madame Howland was Anglo-Saxon except her name. An American fell in love with this beautiful, well-born French woman about 1860 and decided to marry her. After a very short time, I believe, he realized that the place for this Parisienne was Paris and the place for him America, thereby proving first his good taste and then his good sense. Madame Howland settled down easily into being thus left. She was one of those women who, liking company better than society, sure always of being sought after, chose to stay at home and wait there for her friends. . . .

"Madame Howland's taste and her reading in early youth had been shaped by that magnificent philosopher, that perfect conversationalist, Victor Cousin. . . . He gave her the taste for a certain tone, a certain felicity of speech which was recognizable to the end of her life.

sounded off. "What difference does it make to us if they have shoulders when their faces are old and their necks wrinkled? Women expose themselves quite naked, twisting from side to side to show that they still have shoulderblades! How the Orientals must laugh at us.

"One day at the Opéra," Degas continued, "two ladies were resting their great, fat arms on the velvet railing of their box. Suddenly, from up in the gallery, came the cry 'Down with that ham!' Nobody understood. Again the plaintive voice from the gallery: 'Down with that ham!' The audience began to whisper, trying to understand. Finally they caught sight of the fat arms and hooted. The ladies were forced to withdraw.

"What would an Oriental say coming into a bourgeois salon and seeing naked cows sitting on chairs while their husbands, who have made a neat little fortune in business, stand by half-hidden in doorways? The mere fact of being a woman's husband obliges him to haul her from one salon to another quite naked. — If you could have seen Madame de Fleury that year at Diennay! I sat next to her at dinner one evening; she was *décolletée!* And even though I am rather surfeited with such things, I couldn't keep from looking at her arms, her shoulders, everything —. She said, 'Are you staring at me?'

Free and lively, the lessons of the eloquent philosopher had instructed without burdening her, ripened her without making her the least bit pedantic....

"During the Second Empire she lived in the rue Cambon near the boulevards. But she tired of this locality and moved over towards Montmartre, drawn there by several friends....

"Gustave Moreau came often, but was a visitor rather than a friend. His conversation, like his painting, was a little solemn, precious, ornate, stilted; often, however, it was great and very beautiful. Nevertheless it did not suit the taste of our friends. 'That Moreau,' Degas would say impatiently, making fun of his ancient heroes overloaded with jewels, 'he would like us to believe that the gods wore watch-chains.' Degas was an intimate at Madame Howland's, as were my father and her neighbor Cavé, Charles Haas, Jacques-Emile Blanche, Robert de Montesquiou, and a few witty women. . . ." Daniel Halévy, *Pays Parisiens.*

" 'Good Lord, Madame,' I replied, 'I wish I could do otherwise.' It was a mixture of impertinence and flattery. And there, at the other end of the table, sat Monsieur de Fleury who could say nothing because he had lost all his money gambling. . . .' "

There was talk of the mistress of a Monsieur Cahen, a woman whom Degas had known slightly. When Straus[6] spoke of her robust health, her firm skin, Degas said enthusiastically, "She is common." And he added, "It is among the common people that you find grace." These axioms, which written down sound Proudhonesque, Degas says so unpretentiously that I may well have been the only person to hear them.

A propos of Jules Ferry who is growing a beard to outwit the caricaturists: "A man should be ugly," Degas said. "Sometimes when people spoke of hunchbacks or cripples, poor Manet used to say, 'That has its *chic!* That has its *chic!* ' "

There followed some talk between Papa, Mama, Meilhac[7] and Degas about the charm of Manet's nature. He once dined at our house; after dinner they were going to the Gymnase where Pierson was playing in a black dress with pink flowers. This dress had tempted Manet. He wanted to paint her portrait. But it seems that she was so horrified when Manet showed her several portraits of women he had painted that she fled and never returned.[8]

6. Emile Straus, the second husband of Geneviève Halévy Bizet, widow of the composer, was a connection of the Rothschild family, a wealthy lawyer, and counsel for the *Société des Auteurs.*

7. Henri Meilhac (1831–1897), who started his career as a writer for *La Vie Parisienne* and other humorous magazines, collaborated with Ludovic Halévy in the authorship of more than forty comedies and many libretti for Offenbach's operettas as well as the libretto for Bizet's *Carmen.* Meilhac, a confirmed Parisian bachelor, expert at billiards, happiest in the society of ingenues, was a high-strung, restless man who could never bear to sit still through an entire rehearsal.

8. Blanche Pierson, who started acting at the age of 11 in 1853, was noted for her beauty and her gift for light comedy. She became a member of the Comédie-Française in 1886 and acted at that theatre until her death in 1919. The following note to Manet was probably written soon after her visit to his studio. "Monday, 22 July. In a few days I shall stop playing and go away for six weeks leave. When I re-

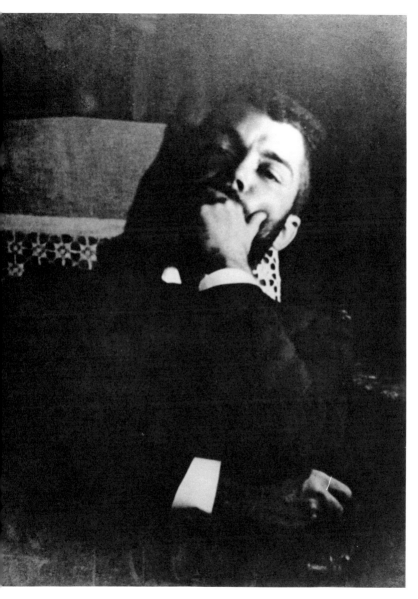

Daniel Halévy in his early twenties.
Photograph by Degas.

Courtesy of Madame Joxe.

Madame Ludovic Halévy. Photograph by Degas.

Courtesy of Madame Joxe.

Degas attacked my uncle Taschereau who reads two books a day. "Don't read," he said. "You only do it out of laziness to avoid thinking. A man should be able to spend hours by his hearth, watching the fire burn, thinking over cherished thoughts — one must have one's own personal thoughts." — I tell it badly, but he spoke very emphatically with something of the fury of a blind man who *can't* read.

17 January 1891
I am reminded of a remark of Degas to Gérôme[9] who said to him: "An artist is always objective." "Objective!" Degas replied. "What about the Italian Primitives who represented the softness of lips by hard strokes and who made eyes come to life by cutting the lids as if with a scissors; and what about the long hands, the thin wrists of Botticelli? Where is your objectivity in art?"

22 January 1891
Yesterday at dinner Jacques Blanche, Taschereau, Meilhac, Degas, us — delightful. Four is the maximum for dinner guests. After dinner Degas talked to us about Ingres. Abraham Dreyfus, who came in during the evening, wondered whether the phrase *good* writer or *brilliant* writer should be put on a tombstone.
"Do you want me to tell you a little story about the word *good?*" Degas asked. "It was the only time I talked to Ingres. I

---

turn I shall have the pleasure of writing to you to find out whether your work will still permit your painting my portrait this autumn." Unpublished letter in collection of editor.
9. Jean-Leon Gérôme (1824–1904), perhaps the most successful academic painter of his day, was an active enemy of the Impressionists. He tried at the Paris World's Fair of 1900 to bar the President of the Republic from entering the Impressionist exhibition by shouting, "Halt, Mr. President, here you see France disgraced." After a visit to Constantinople in 1875 he painted many pictures of harems, slave markets, etc. His nudes, Henry James remarked, seemed "more than naked."
When Gérôme criticized Degas's painting *Spartan Girls Challenging Spartan Boys to Combat*, Degas replied, "I suppose it isn't Turkish enough for you, Gérôme."

was sent to go and ask him for the loan of a picture for an exhibition. And I took advantage of the opportunity to tell him that I was doing some painting, that I was in love with art and would like his advice. The pictures that hung in his studio are still photographed in my mind. 'Draw lines, young man,' he said to me, 'draw lines; whether from memory or after nature. Then you will be a good artist.' "

"The curious thing about that interview," said Jacques Blanche, "is that in the history of painting you will be Ingres's pupil."

"Is that the only time you saw him?" someone asked.

"No, but the only time he spoke to me. I saw him again at one of his exhibitions. He was there with an old gentleman. In front of a classical painting, the old man said, 'Still in love with antiquity, Monsieur Ingres?' Ingres remained impassive. 'Yes.' Then they stopped in front of a woman, an odalisque that is at Chantilly —"

Jacques Blanche interrupted: "It's an improper painting."

"Improper? — You have a singular turn of mind, young Blanche — The old gentleman stopped, quivering with pleasure: 'And now for the pleasing subject, eh, Monsieur Ingres?' — 'Yes,' Ingres replied, still imperturbable, 'I have more than one brush.' "

Then Degas spoke with admiration of Ingres's wit: "It's curious. There is Delacroix, an admirable artist whose little pamphlets are so dull[1] — You can't, on the other hand, quote a remark of Ingres that isn't a masterpiece." And standing in front of Jacques he repeated:

"Form is not in the contour; it lies within the contour.

"Shadow is not an addition to the contour but makes it.

"A reflection on the shadows of the contour is unworthy of the majesty of art.

"One must master the inner structure in order to express the planes.

"Muscles I know; they are my friends. But I have forgotten their names."

1. Delacroix's *Journal* and *Correspondance* had not yet been published. D.H.

Jacques seated, his head thrown back, drank in these words. Jacques with his admirable artist's temperament, a talent for writing, a talent for music, a talent for painting — and unable to achieve success in anything, knowing it and growing embittered. In Paris he has distractions; he sees people. But at Dieppe he lives shut in, dying of his vain labors. He literally makes himself ill.

(I am not changing these lines written seventy years ago. They express the disparaging opinion of Jacques-Emile Blanche held by his contemporaries.[2] The versatility of his gifts, his mordant wit, the great fortune he enjoyed without pretentions, engendered an ill-will from which he suffered to the end of his life. I am convinced today that there was great injustice in all this. Jacques-Emile Blanche was caustic but not malicious. In choosing the models that he did, he created a collection of portraits of a society that is recognized today as representing the elite of both France and England. After his death in the spring of 1944, the retrospective exhibition of his works at the Orangerie silenced his detractors. The thirty canvases assembled in the museum at Rouen show him to have been a fine French portraitist, perhaps the last. We are indebted to him for an excellent likeness of Degas.[3])

At dinner, Degas was good, too. Jacques had told him that Mirbeau[4] was going to launch a very distinguished painter called Gauguin,[5] as he had launched Maeterlinck.

2.   An analytical defense of Jacques-Emile Blanche, as man and painter, was written by Marcel Proust, in his Preface to Blanche's *Propos de Peintre: De David à Degas,* Paris, 1919.

3.   This portrait was painted on the condition that there should be only one sitting and that it should never be shown in Degas's lifetime. "It will amuse me to see how you will make out in a single day," Degas said. The portrait was destroyed in a fire.

4.   Octave Mirbeau (1850–1917), playwright, novelist, and journalist, was one of the earliest defenders of the Impressionist painters. He wrote regularly for the *Figaro* and also for the anarchist paper *Révolte* from 1890 to 1894, when his anarchist sympathies were checked by the assassination of President Carnot. Mirbeau was also an early and consistent Dreyfusard.

5.   Gauguin wrote to his friend Monfried from Papeete in 1898, "I am very happy that you have met Degas and that in trying to be

"Who is this Gauguin?" someone asked Degas.

"A lad who is dying of hunger and whom I esteem profoundly as an artist. But I don't understand how despair can drive a man to knock at the door of the *Figaro.*"

And when there was talk of a woman whom Degas had found pretty:

"You liked her because she was ugly, admit it," Mama said.

"Ah, yes, that's always the point. To be a woman, and not be pretty."

"That happens frequently," someone said.

"I said: be a woman," Degas repeated, and added that the chief charm in a woman is to know how to listen.

He talked about someone who had gone to farm in Canada.

"I was very happy to see him escape from journalism."

"Was he a journalist?"

"He might have become one."

30 January 1891

Last night Degas talked comparatively little. He spoke of Jacques Blanche's studio.[6] "Oh," he said, "what light! My eyes immediately felt rested. If only I could afford a separate studio."

"But the light there is so soft because the windows are slightly frosted and tinted. You could do that."

---

useful to me something helpful to you has resulted. Oh, yes, Degas is supposed to be *ill-tempered* and caustic. (I am, too, says Z——) But he is not that way to those whom he *judges* worthy of his attention and esteem. His heart and his mind are instinctive. . . . Both in his *talent* and in his *conduct* Degas is a rare example of what the artist should be. His colleagues and admirers are the powers that be — Bonnat, Puvis, Antonin Proust, etc. — but he has *never* asked anyone for *anything*. No one *ever heard* anything nasty, unscrupulous, or in any way mean *about him*. Art and dignity." *Lettres de Paul Gauguin à Georges-Daniel de Monfried,* Paris, 1920.

6. In 1883 Oscar Wilde wrote to Jacques-Emile Blanche, "I so enjoy seeing your studio with its peacock-blue door and the little green and gold room. For me it is a fresh oasis of beauty in the Louis XVI desert that I find in Paris." *The Letters of Oscar Wilde,* Ed. Rupert Hart-Davis, London, 1962.

"Yes. There are people," he said brusquely, "who claim that tinted glass is bad because it changes the color. No!! If I had the time and the means to write I would explain how stupid that is. — There is a painter called Humbert who takes pupils. He tells them: You must get the color of the model. And he sets up the canvas right beside the model. To do a thing like that is so stupid that it isn't even worth thinking about." He was silent for a while, and then he added quickly, "What I mean is that everything in a picture is the inter-relationships. We paint the sun with the yolk of egg. Go put your canvas alongside the sun!"

1891 (Probably February)

This evening General Duhesme and Degas for dinner. Duhesme was just back from maneuvers. He talked about them. Degas, excessively patriotic, did nothing but listen. As a matter of fact Degas likes nothing better than to be silent. After Duhesme left Degas talked. Recently he has been having dealings with artisans in their homes. It has to do with mountings for canes, which are his craze at the moment.

"I like to see the families of the workingmen in the Marais," he said. "You go into these wretched-looking houses with great, wide doors, and you find bright rooms, meticulously clean. You can see them through the open doors from the hall. Everybody is lively; everybody is working. And these people have none of the servility of a merchant in his shop. Their society is delightful."

Degas also told us about his plans for work. "For a whole year I shall devote myself to drawing." I have often heard Degas express a (relative) contempt for everything that is preponderantly color. But he has a special way of translating his thoughts into gestures. With him a gesture is not a crude expression of an idea. When he talks he always involuntarily searches for the ideal line, the curve identical with his thought. One day he said to my mother, "Louise, I would like to do your portrait; your features are *excessively outlined.*"

He railed against the administration of the Louvre. Recently some workmen who were replastering a vault let some plaster fall on the *Pilgrims of Emmaüs,* "one of the masterpieces of the human spirit. What kind of curators do they have there? Do they like pictures? What is Kaempfen? A journalist! Oh, *'la gent de lettre!'* as Proudhon said." And he repeated several times, as if to himself, *"La gent de lettre! La gent de lettre!"*[7]

Afterwards he talked about old things and old times, of the superior workmanship of the ancient guilds, of the quarrel between the painters' guild and the Academy; and in this connection he mentioned the rules of admission and particularly the admission of Watteau.

In order to become a member of the Academy a painter had to submit a painting to the jury which after several days' consideration voted and decided. But Watteau's picture was not ready until the voting day. However, this did not bother him. He simply placed his painting in the corridor leading to the voting-hall. The jurymen arrived, saw the canvas, and waived any formality. Watteau was accepted as a member.

While saying this Degas stretched out his hand; my mother, thinking that he was about to leave, took it. But he only meant to express by this gesture the simplicity of the act, its 'graciousness,' to use a word the meaning of which he has practically renewed. (Degas habitually used this gesture after telling a story that he considered significant. Or else he would say, "What?" in a loud voice.) After a moment's silence he added, "Today it doesn't happen so easily. It's done through the newspapers." Again, after another brief silence, he said very quickly, very low, "You will never see me there..."

1891 (Probably February)

Cavé, who lunched with us today, had recently gone to a velocipede competition to which Degas had summoned him to see two dancers from the Opéra doing stunts on tricycles. And Cavé told us how funny Degas's attitude was towards these little

7. *"Gent de lettre"* is an obsolete, pejorative expression which means a sheeplike herd of writers.

54

creatures, and their attitude towards him. He finds them all charming, treats them as though they were his own children, makes excuses for anything they do, and laughs at everything they say. On the other hand, they absolutely venerate him and the most insignificant little *"rat"* would give a good deal to please Degas.

This evening, Degas for dinner. He told us a remark he had made about Jean-Paul Laurens.[8] It was at an exhibition in front of a historical painting: a desperate Merovingian woman is rushing out of a house which forms the background of the picture. The whole thing is a clash of colors and on the frame there is a historic notation: some Gunslwinde or other escaping . . . "So," said Degas, "you think you know why this young woman is fleeing so fast? You don't, though. It is because she is out of key with her background. — I think," Degas added, "that this remark was repeated to Jean-Paul Laurens. Because one day I asked a model where he was posing and he replied, 'At J.-P. Laurens. I even told him one day that I was posing for you and he made a gesture . . .' as if he had stepped on a snake," Degas concluded.

At dinner, after some sort of burst of temper on his part, my mother said to him jokingly, "You are always having to be told how stupid you are."

"I don't care," he said, "as long as I can always keep on drawing a little."

March 1891

Degas, particularly irritated by painters, by Detaille[9] who was the most eager of all of them for the exhibition and who,

8. Jean-Paul Laurens (1838–1921) was a prolific and successful historical painter. Among his many works were *The Death of Cato, The Death of Tiberius, The Death of the Duc d'Enghien, The Death of St. Geneviève,* and the ceiling of the Théâtre de l'Odeon.

9. Edouard Detaille (1848–1912) devoted his life to painting the French army and to being a social success. His battle-scenes resembled orderly maneuvers and even under fire his fighting men looked as clean and neat as toy soldiers.

smelling a rat, backed out today and declared that he will not exhibit.

"So at last we know what painters are worth!" Degas complained.

"But, after all, what has kept you from seeing Detaille's real function? He is a purveyor of military equipment."

20 March 1891

Degas at dinner yesterday. But why repeat anecdotes? Only because certain people will say that he was ill-tempered and envious, I merely want to report that after having made fun of Bonnat he refused to repeat his epigrams, saying: "No, I am talking nonsense. I am making fun of an old comrade who is very kind and whom I like very much."[1]

Then this remark about Madame Ganderax: "Yes, I like her a lot. She is just ugly and common enough to suit me."

24 April 1891

Last night before dinner the talk was about *Antonia*.[2] Meilhac was there and said, "I am told that the lines were 'assonan-

1. I several times heard Degas speak affectionately of Bonnat. And I shall repeat here a remark of Bonnat's that someone told me: "I don't like to spend much time talking to Degas; if I do, I am tempted after I leave him to change my way of painting." D.H.

Léon Bonnat (1833–1922), one of the most highly paid portrait painters of his day, spent a large part of his fortune collecting paintings which he left to the Museum of Bayonne, his birthplace.

" 'To achieve the honor of being portrayed by Bonnat,' a contemporary journalist wrote, 'you had to prepare for it by fasting, prayer, and every sort of austerity. Then . . . you must order a Bonnat portrait-costume; there are special models. You must get yourself recommended by a General, a Minister or an Ambassador, and then, but only then, Monsieur Bonnat will consent to paint you standing upright, stiff as a post, bright as crystal, and lit from above.' " Henri Perruchot, *Toulouse-Lautrec,* Cleveland and New York, 1960.

2. *Antonia* was a symbolist play written in rhythmic prose by Edouard Dujardin. He had rented a theatre for a performance of his play and had scattered invitations far and wide to make sure of a large audience. There was great curiosity about it, and carriages crowded the rue de la Chaussée-d'Antin and the rue Lafayette. The actors wore frock coats and evening dress. The audience listened to the first few

ciated' . . ." The remark was quoted in the *Figaro* this very morning. And Degas, who liked the play, was late; he didn't arrive until dinner was half over. And what stupid statements were uttered in the meantime! They made me furious. "But I assure you," Degas said, "it was not unpleasant; and the first two acts were very pretty, weren't they, Daniel?" "Very pretty!" I exclaimed with an enthusiasm intensified by my irritation. Everybody laughed loudly. This bothered me very little; but after dinner I was happy to see that my juvenile enthusiasm had not displeased Degas. I think he found it *gracieux,* a charming expression of his . . .

I said to him, "Monsieur, you have made copies of pictures in the Louvre, haven't you? Where are they?"

"Yes, my dear Daniel," he replied with such affection that it still makes me happy. But my question was not satisfactorily answered. I learned only one thing, that his copy of Poussin's *Rape of the Sabine Women* belongs to an associate of his friends the Rouarts. Where are the copies of the primitives, which must be admirable?

30 April 1891

Degas dined with us this evening. For a long time after dinner he chatted with Jacques Blanche; they talked about lithography, technical processes. They launched violent attacks against Salons, juries, art criticism. Degas said that he greatly admired Delacroix's lithographs.

After my aunt left, most brilliantly dressed for a ball at Madame de Wagram's,[3] Degas said: "I once went to a charity ball. All the faubourg Saint-Germain was there: Women in shabby

---

scenes, but soon they started whispering and the evening ended in a wave of hysterical laughter. D.H.

3. Madame Emile Straus, widow of Georges Bizet, the daughter of the composer of *La Juive,* Fromental Halévy, was a first cousin and very close friend of Daniel Halévy's father. Noted for her charm, her wit, and her salon, she served Marcel Proust as partial model for the Duchesse de Guermantes. For Proust's difficulties in arriving at the Princesse de Wagram's ball, see the preface to J. E. Blanche's *De David à Degas.*

dresses covered with diamonds. It was frightfully smart. They didn't take the trouble to dress up like actresses."

(I am reminded of a remark of Degas that seemed to be connected with this same ball. "Women in the high society of the past," he told me one day, "had the kind of easy manners that we can't imagine today. One evening I found myself at a ball where there were women belonging to that former world. I was rather alone. One of them was sitting in a chair near me, resting. Suddenly she looked up. 'Monsieur,' she said, 'I left my fan on a little table in that corner of the salon. It would be very kind of you to fetch it and give it to me.' Never would a woman of the bourgeoisie ask a man whom she didn't know to wait on her.")

17 May 1891

Night before last Degas came for dinner. We were downstairs at Grandmother's when he dropped in. Papa was there. They talked about the Carrières[4] at the Salon.

"How do you explain," Papa asked naïvely, "that color of Carrière's? Does he see things in clouds?"

"Monsieur Halévy," Degas replied, "you are talking nonsense. There is one Liebreich[5] in England who is convinced that an artist's originality lies in a special contexture of the eye. He has discovered lenses that transform all landscapes into Turners. I am convinced that these differences in vision are of no importance. One sees as one wishes to see. It's false; and it is that falsity that constitutes art." . . .

Degas also said: "I found myself at dinner yesterday next to a brilliant general. He talked about painting. 'My wife and I,' he said, 'went to the Salon. And all prejudice aside, we agreed that there were twenty pictures there worthy of scrutiny. First of all,

4. Eugène Carrière (1849–1906) painted chiefly mothers and babies, family groups, and an occasional portrait of a friend such as Edmond de Goncourt or Gustave Geffroy. His technique was the merging of varied colors in a single tone, the dissolving of sharp contours in a smoke-hued mist. His remark, "Let us restore to that beautiful word 'sentimentality' all its high and happy significance," is perhaps a clue to his approach to art.

5. R. Liebreich, ophthalmic surgeon at St. Thomas's Hospital, lectured before the Royal Institution of Great Britain, March 8, 1872,

aside from that masterly canvas by M. Rochegrosse with its wonderfully skillful drawing, its aerial perspective, its remarkable taste in the choice of accessories, in their placing, in the grouping of the whole composition — masterly erudition — ' 'Good Lord, Monsieur,' I said, 'there is a way of doing without all that. It is a simple and curious way; it is just to have talent. With talent there is no need of masterly skill in drawing nor of aerial perspective nor — ' He was flabbergasted."

Ah, if Degas knew that I was writing all this down! George Moore has just done an extremely eulogistic article about him — *exagéré*, as he said to us one day in his awkward French. Degas immediately quarreled with him. Moore then wrote asking us to pacify Degas a little. We knew how useless it was, but when Moore came back to Paris we asked Degas whether he would be willing to dine with him. Degas said no and again went off into a wild rage against anything resembling a journalist.

"Those people trap you in your bed, strip off your shirt, corner you in the street, and when you complain, they say: 'You belong to the public.' "

Thursday 1 October 1891

Degas: "Women think in little packages. I understand nothing about the way their minds work. They put every subject into an envelope, label it and it's finished ... little packages ... little packages. — I had Forain for dinner the other day. He came to keep me company."

"His wife, too?"

(Scornfully) "She was unwell."

"Wasn't she really?"

"How does anyone know? Women have invented the word 'unwell'; it doesn't mean anything."

31 January 1892

Degas, after vituperating against writers, mentioned some detail having to do with diamond-cutting. "The conversation of

---

on "Turner and Mulready — On the Effect of certain Faults of Vision on Painting, with especial Reference to their Works."

specialists is so enjoyable," he said. "You don't understand it but it's charming. Haas told me that he once was fellow-member of an arts commission with two mathematicians. He was sitting in front of them and out of boredom listened to their conversation. They were talking about the present state of mathematics and one of them said, 'The square on the hypotenuse will always be young.' "

This reminded me of another remark by a mathematician. He was leafing through an algebra book by Lermite and looking at the pages covered with figures, he said, "You can immediately recognize a page of Lermite's."

Ganderax[6] recently did an article in which he mentioned Degas. And Degas was characteristically irritated. Ganderax found out about it and wrote him a letter of apology. Degas's reply was adamant: "In the future don't bother me any more." My father teased him about his mania[7] and repeated to him some rather good remarks of Mounet-Sully.[8] In reply to Jules Claretie, director of the Comédie-Française, who criticized him for speaking so low that no one could hear him, the actor said, "Do I act for them? Let them buy the text and follow it. The way I act is right." And when Claretie complained at having

6. "Louis Ganderax, a man of great wit and extreme cultivation was the embodiment of what in the old days in France was called *l'honnête homme*. This very exacting integrity took the form of a scrupulousness, pushed in his later years to the limits of neurasthenia. As editor of the *Revue de Paris* he applied his scruples to correcting the proof of every number. These proof-sheets finally became prodigious examples of erudite and grammatical subtlety. He knew it, he apologized for it, and I remember having received from him proofs overloaded with observations which he himself called his 'professional hyperaesthesia.' Things came to such a pass that in order to rid himself of his scruples he gave up the editorship of the *Revue de Paris*. D.H." quoted in notes of *Letters of Marcel Proust,* Ed. Mina Curtiss, New York, 1949.

7. "Indeed there was something in the nature of a mania here. Degas had known Ganderax for a long time and certainly appreciated his scrupulousness. There was surely no modicum of indiscretion in his mention of Degas. D.H." Footnote in *Lettres de Degas*.

8. Mounet-Sully (1841–1916) was the outstanding tragic actor at the Comédie-Française from 1872 for over forty years.

been forced to rehearse a repertory piece five times, Mounet-Sully replied, "My dear sir, permit me to tell you that one should always be in rehearsal."

"That's what you think," my mother said to Degas.

"No, I think a man must work for just a few people. The rest don't matter."

12 February 1892

Degas told us this anecdote about Barbey d'Aurevilly and Mlle Read.[9]

9. Jules Amédée Barbey d'Aurevilly (1808–1889) was born in Normandy, studied law at Caen where he fell under the spell of the exiled, slightly mad Beau Brummell. Barbey, also an admirer of Lord Byron and Baudelaire, practiced dandyism and Don Juanism throughout his life. A prolific writer of novels, short stories, and criticism, he is remembered today largely for *Les Diaboliques*.

A contemporary journalist gives a succinct picture of Barbey in 1875. "Barbey d'Aurevilly lovingly detracts the works of his colleagues to attract attention to himself, parades the streets in costumes that cause youngsters to ask, 'Papa, is that gentleman in masquerade?' He wears a broad-brimmed top-hat, a tight-waisted frock-coat with huge cuffs that dazzle passers-by and writes in different colored inks to suit the mood of each piece.

"All this is trickery, not talent; know-how, not knowledge. Will no one be kind enough to tell this word-slinger that originality is not achieved by striving for it?

"M. Barbey d'Aurevilly is monarchist and clerical. We need hardly say that he has already made converts . . . to the Republic and to free-thinking." Pierre Véron, *Le Panthéon de Poche*, Paris, 1875.

Degas made two brilliant drawings of Barbey which are reproduced in *Croquis de Degas*, Introduction by Daniel Halévy, Paris, n.d.

Louise Read was the last of Barbey d'Aurevilly's many *amies*. Introduced by the sister of a friend who thought Barbey had arrived at an age where he needed sisterly care, Mlle Read was in her forties. Of Scottish Puritan descent, she dressed drably, tastelessly, wearing shoddy materials that frequently emitted the odor of cats.

"Barbey started out being recalcitrant. He admitted that he had 'a secret horror of devotion.' But since he had foibles, they were exploited. . . . Mlle Read could read proof — Barbey couldn't stand a single mistake in his articles — , would see his publishers, go to bookbinders, to editorial offices, and would keep his accounts. She pam-

"X—— was at Barbey's one morning about nine o'clock. Mlle Read was not there. When she came in, Barbey d'Aurevilly said to her, 'Mademoiselle, I would like to know how things stand between us. Are you taking care of me or aren't you? If you aren't, get out.' Mlle Read without speaking went into the next room and started dusting, cleaning, moving furniture around. 'Young man,' said Barbey d'Aurevilly in his stentorian voice, 'that will teach you how to be loved.' X——, rather indignant, stopped on his way out to tell Mlle Read that she was really very kind to look after such a boor. 'When we are alone,' she replied, 'he is charming.' "

19 February 1892

Degas told us that Mallarmé came to see him the other day on behalf of Roujon, the new director of the Beaux-Arts, to sound him out and ask whether he would be willing to give a picture to the Luxembourg. He told us the charming way in which he responded to this approach.

"I said no, certainly not. Those people want me to believe that I am successful. Successful, what does that mean? Either you always are, or never. What is success? To be hung on the wall between a lady by Bouguereau[1] and a slave market by Toto Girod? When each one of us sticks to his last and forms his own small group of admirers, why does the administration want to meddle in our affairs? I pay them my taxes. What have my pictures got to do with them? No. They have to interfere in everything. They have the fine-arts chessboard on their desk and

---

pered his gourmet appetite . . . kept his multicolored ink-wells filled and sharpened his quill-pens. She was both practical and literary, and carried out her work with such ecstatic fervor that she ended by touching Barbey's heart. At first he had disdainfully called her 'la Read,' but gradually she became indispensable to him. . . . There was one gentler bond between them. Like Baudelaire and Huysmans, Barbey liked to be surrounded by cats and his Démonette was cherished by Mlle Read." Elisabeth de Gramont, *Barbey d'Aurevilly,* Paris, 1946.

1. Adolphe-William Bouguereau (1825–1905) was a successful academic painter noted particularly for the slickness and eroticism of his Bacchantes, nymphs, and satyrs. Degas and his friends used to say that an overfinished slick piece of painting was *"Bouguereauté."*

we artists are the pieces. They shove this pawn one way, that one another. I am not a pawn. I don't want to be pushed."

My father lost his temper and treated Degas as though he were a fool. "Do you know what you act like? A man who is embittered and thinks recognition has come too late."

"Bitter? But I am very happy. Everybody knows that."

"Only those who know you personally."

"You have no perspective in these things. The fact is that if I were hung in the Luxembourg I'd feel as though I were being arrested. *Success!* The end of progress! Success! What does it mean? How do you succeed? (Later on Degas would say, "In my day, people didn't 'succeed'.") I do not wish to be caught by the *beaux-arts* policemen or by that officer of the guard named Roujon."

27 February 1892

Degas came to lunch the other day as lively as a cricket. He was delighted by the spectacle of the dissension between painters which the Salon always produces. Boldini's[2] despair and Helleu's arrogance, because Mirbeau mentioned one but not the other, enchanted him. My father used this as a pretext to tell him that Roujon was angry because Degas vilified him wherever he went. "I saw him," said my father, "and he spoke to me rather bitterly, saying that he could see nothing criminal about having asked you for a painting. I replied that you were always like that and people laughed at you for it. But some day when Roujon is at the Opéra I'll take you there and introduce you to each other."

2. Giovanni Boldini (1845–1931), Italian by birth, came to Paris for the International Exposition of 1867 with a group of English aristocrats whom he had met in Florence and who introduced him to their friends in Paris. His success as a fashionable portrait painter was immediate and life-long. His friendship with Degas whom he met in 1873 continued intermittently for many years. Soon after the International Exposition of 1889, at which Boldini's portrait of Verdi caused much talk, Degas and he went to Spain together. In a letter to Boldini discussing their plans Degas wrote, "You will travel incognito, won't you?"

"I ask nothing better," Degas replied. "But I don't want you to defend me the way you do by saying that I am a crazy old man. You must say that I am a philosopher. Not a madman, a philosopher, an old philosopher. Tell him, 'Degas is considered an eccentric; if you tried to argue with him he would silence you in two words. He is a —' "

He intended repeating the word "philosopher," but he was laughing so hard he couldn't speak. Yet that very morning he had to return a letter that he couldn't read because he is losing his eyesight so rapidly. He told us this with no sign of distress and I have never seen him so gay. It is nothing more than the pride of a man who doesn't wish to be an object of pity and who wants to find in himself the strength to live joyfully. Yet he doubtless knows that in two years he will be blind. Degas is not a man to harbor illusions nor to protect himself from the truth. But the sadness he suppresses certainly explains much of the violence of his reflexes as a solitary old man.

17 April 1892

It is now considered abusive to say to someone: You are gay. Would the Greeks have understood such a state of mind? I think even in the eighteenth century sad people were rather scorned.

This feeling is justified. Without doubt most superior people, except Degas, are sad. The ones who are gay are "little people," people without character, without individuality, with little joys and little sorrows. The only people who can live in times like these without losing their strength and their gaiety are artists, and of these the most marvelous character is Degas. Artists live in a separate world; they pay little heed to the restrictions of the world outside.

Leisure is an art, the highest of all the arts. Uneducated people can only work with their hands, twiddle their thumbs, or do odd jobs. The need for an intellectual to set himself a task is equally a sign of vulgarity. The right kind of man is as at home with his mind as with his hands. That is what Degas meant

Daniel Halévy and his mother. Photograph by Degas.
Courtesy of Bibliothèque Nationale.

Self portrait of Degas with his maid Zoé.
Courtesy of Bibliothèque Nationale.

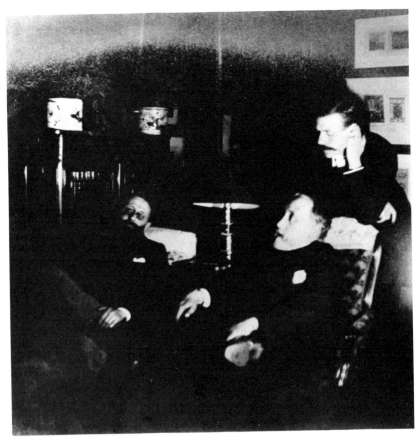

Uncle Taschereau, Jacques-Emile Blanche, and Degas.
Photograph by Degas.

Courtesy of Madame Joxe.

the other day when he said, "Leisure is the loveliest thing in the world when one doesn't suffer from it."

Friendship is necessarily jealous. If one is not jealous of men it is because over and above one's friendship for other men there are many additional elements: a sharing of ideas, intellectual admiration, and the advantages of an exchange of ideas. Admiration is the death-knell of affection. I have no true affection for Degas, whom I have every reason to love, because I admire him too much.

September 1892

Degas came to dinner yesterday with his niece, a young American girl[3] whom he invited to visit him on condition that she never ask him to escort her anywhere. Actually this young girl strolls around Paris from morning to night; after dinner Degas takes her to the theatre but never any place but Batignolles, Moncey, or Montmartre.[4]

After dinner the conversation turned to the *Thousand and One Nights* and Degas asked me if I had any news of the English edition I was supposed to have found out about. I told him that it was in fifteen volumes and cost nine hundred francs.

"I thought it was twelve hundred," Degas replied. "Are you going to buy it?"

We protested.

"But why not?"

"For nine hundred francs? How you go on!"

"Nine hundred francs! What difference does that make to you? What does money mean anyway? Does it exist? When I want something it's that thing that exists. Money! Money! You know what? I'll buy this translation with my money, my nine hundred francs. What difference does it make to me? I'll do two

3. The young American girl was probably a member of the New Orleans branch of the family.

4. At Batignolles and Montmartre romantic melodramas were played; at Moncey early nineteenth-century Italian and French operettas.

or three more pastels and they'll pay for it. I'll pay them their nine hundred francs and then, at home, I'll look at my fifteen volumes and it will make me happy, very happy. Then you will see me coming here with a volume under my arm and you will read me some of it. I shall have them, I shall have them, and the joke is that I shan't even be able to read them myself."

At that moment he would have bought them outright. But he asked Elie to find him a set at a reduced price in London, and this calmed him a little. "But I could pay for them," he said. "I have twenty-one landscapes."

We all protested. "Twenty-one landscapes? But you have never done any! Not twenty-one?"

"Yes, twenty-one landscapes."[5]

"But how did you happen to do them?"

"They are the fruit of my travels this summer. I would stand at the door of the coach and as the train went along I could see things vaguely. That gave me the idea of doing some landscapes. There are twenty one."

"What kind are they? Vague things?"

"Perhaps."

"Reflections of your soul?" my father asked. "Amiel said, 'A landscape is a reflection of the soul.' Do you like that definition?"

"A reflection of my eyesight," Degas replied. "We painters do not use such pretentious language."

In the street that led from his studio to our house the sidewalks were being rebuilt. The stonemasons shaped the granite with axe strokes as sculptors do to achieve an exact, sometimes delicate shape. Degas would talk to the masons, handle the chips, and hold them up to focus on their form in the light. One day at our house, before sitting down at table, he had us admire the shape of one of these chips. "I shall make a landscape," he said, "and call it *Le Cap de la belle épaule.*"

5. These landscapes were shown at the Durand-Ruel galleries in October, 1892. They were admired by Pissarro who mentioned them in a letter to his son Lucien, October 2, 1892.

The slightest discovery of this kind makes him savor the possibility of a challenge and enchants him.

October 1892

Degas has been here very little lately. I wonder whether he has seen more of his other friends. I believe that for the time being he is isolating himself. His eyes are getting worse and worse; he wears a special kind of glasses that bother him a great deal. All this depresses him and I suspect that he stays alone so as to hide this melancholy he has fought so hard.

Last month he must have stopped work altogether while trying to get used to his new glasses. (He was alone in Belgium for a week without even being able to read a time-table.)

August 1893

Degas, who came to see our house,[6] ran into his friend Rouart with whom Papa renewed his acquaintance. I talked music with Degas. "He's a bore! He's a bore (naturally Wagner) with his Grail and his Father Parsifal. The human voice was not made to sing Greek roots."

Rouart's younger son is studying painting under Degas. They went off to talk together. When he came back, Degas said, "You see, you paint a monochrome ground, something absolutely unified; you put a little color on it, a touch here, a touch there, and you will see how little it takes to make it come to life."

Elie and I walked back with Degas from the Rouarts' at Queue-en-Brie to Sucy. "It is in this part of the country," he told us, "that Napoleon gave a lot of property to his generals — Marshal Lefebvre for example, and an old colonel called Aversin whose sons Rouart and I used to play with. The old man had been a full-fledged Colonel of the Guard. — He'd seen plenty," Degas added in an amused voice. (It is extraordinary to think

6. This was the *Haute Maison* at Sucy-en-Brie that my father bought in 1893. D.H.

how close we modern Parisians are to one of the heroic ages of human history.)

"They used to tell lots of stories here in the country about Marshal Lefebvre," Degas continued. "They said that a friend of his visiting the château remarked, 'You are very lucky to have earned a house in which to end your days.' 'My friend,' said Lefebvre, 'do you want my house? It is yours. All you have to do is go down into the courtyard. I will arm twenty of the boys from the village who will shoot at you. If you survive, the château is yours. That is how I earned it.'

"I was also told of games of lotto in the evening at the Marshal's. They were played in his wife's bedroom. Around ten o'clock she would withdraw from the game. 'Don't look,' she would say. 'I am going to undress now.' Then she would carry on a conversation from her bed."

August 1893

M. Blanche[7] is dead. He was mad like all his contemporaries and ridiculous looking. Tall, imposing, like a doctor in a play, he always wore a long frock coat and a broad-brimmed high silk hat tilted on the back of his head. At home he invariably wore a skull cap and talked like an oracle. "Monsieur Blanche," Degas says, *"always full face."* Entering, leaving, chatting first with one person, then another, M. Blanche was *always full face*. His profile was unworthy of a member of the Medical Faculty.

29 November 1894

Degas: terrible injury to his eyes; he protects himself and painfully feigns happiness. His gaiety now comes in fits and starts, and is complicated by anger.

"I have never felt younger than today," he keeps repeating. Last month at the Gauguin sale I sat beside him. Such intensity!

7. Antoine-Emile Blanche (1828–1893), father of the painter Jacques-Emile Blanche and son of the famous alienist Esprit Blanche, was also an alienist. Through the sanitarium in Passy founded by his father passed many distinguished patients, among them Charles Gounod and Guy de Maupassant.

He kept bidding and letting himself be carried away by prices that frightened even him. What's more, he couldn't even see the pictures he bought. He would ask me: "What is it?" and then remember. He bought a copy of the *Olympia* that he had never seen. He would lean over to his neighbors and ask, "Is it beautiful?"

Aunt Geneviève, who was having Degas to dinner, invited me to keep him company a little. He is very sad.

This autumn he has spent a number of evenings with us taking photographs. His mind is so active, his thoughts are so painful that he is continually swamped by them. His art fills his days, but in the evening he needs something else. He has been obsessed by the techniques of engraving, of poetry; he developed a passion for *canes* and all kinds of wood. He became passionately anti-Semitic, violent against the Louvre. But these last passions were too real; they embittered him. This year he has become enamored of photography, and as his days are full he takes photographs in the evening. "Daylight," he says, "is too easy. What I want is difficult — the atmosphere of lamps or moonlight."

Degas did not come to the house for several days. The other evening the bell rang and we heard his slow, heavy footsteps. He stopped, looked at us and didn't speak for a while. Then he said, in a voice he was unable to control, "I am not very cheerful. Marguerite is dead."

Marguerite was his sister; a charming woman, a great friend of my mother's, an excellent musician. She used to sing old Italian songs for her brother. She was married to a M. Fèvre, an architect who speculated in building houses which he couldn't rent. Bankrupt, he left for Buenos Aires with his family where they have been living miserably.

Degas sat down on the sofa. "For the past two months I have been worried," he said. "But I kept hoping. Three days ago I received a telegram. The poor creature is dead. When I bade her goodbye eight years ago I didn't think that it was forever. I always had the notion of going to see them down there. But one does nothing one wants to do. I have been unhappy, depressed the last few days. I haven't gone out. I stopped taking walks and have felt flushed and could do nothing the next day. Besides if I go to bed without talking a walk I think about poor Marguerite and I can't sleep. There will be no services. You remember there were none when our brother died. To have them for her would debase the memory of poor Achille. They will bring Marguerite back. I must find out about all that. Fèvre wrote me that before she died she expressed a certain horror at the idea of staying down there. She was homesick. It was partly that that killed her I am sure. So they will bring her back. It happens that there is one place left in our vault. When Achille died it was full. But our cousin Madame de X—— was there, unclaimed by her son. To make room I wrote to him that I would be grateful if he would have her buried elsewhere. Bartholomé and I went to the exhumation.[8] Her son didn't even come. He is a skunk whom I never see any more," he exclaimed with sudden violence. Then he continued, "I thought that place would be for me. It seems that I was mistaken. Now let's talk about something else."

Suddenly he talked cheerfully about a little girl, one of his models whom he had recommended to Papa for the Conservatoire. But in the middle of a sentence that made us laugh he stopped and, putting his hand to his brow, cried out in the most anguished voice, "Oh, my God!"

Then he talked about two ideas with which at the moment he is preoccupied: the administration of the Louvre and the rejection of the bequest.[9] He spoke sharply, angrily. Finally he

8. Bartholomé's fellow-feeling at this time of mourning calls to mind Degas's great sympathy at the time of the death of Bartholomé's wife. D.H.

9. The Caillebotte bequest. Gustave Caillebotte, a specialist in ship-building and owner of several yachts, a wealthy bachelor and amateur painter, met Monet and Renoir at Argenteuil in the summer of 1874. He became a friend, patron, and colleague of the Impressionists, helped them by buying their paintings. By 1876, when he was only twenty-seven, he had already acquired a large enough collection to cause him to plan its final disposition. He wrote a will, leaving all his

rose and said, "Goodbye, I mustn't go to bed too late and I must take my walk." We went downstairs to the door with him.

Another day (no date)

... Degas talked to me about the Louvre: "What do I want? I want them not to restore the paintings. If you were to scratch a painting you would be arrested. If M. Kaempfen were to restore the *Gioconda* they'd decorate him. ... Time has to take its course with paintings as with everything else, that's the beauty of it. A man who touches a picture ought to be deported. To touch a picture! You don't know what that does to me. These pictures are the joy of my life; they beautify it, they soothe it. To touch a Rembrandt! It's as though — "

We were at the door of his studio. He disappeared.

(Degas stopped talking and disappeared. But I am able to say something he didn't. Rembrandt's *Pilgrims of Emmaüs* had been the cause of great difficulties. When the picture was put back on display after restoration art-lovers could no longer recognize it. In its former state there had been a shadow at the bottom of the painting under the table. This shadow had disappeared. Without it the picture had lost its mystery. When there were complaints the museum directors were supercilious. During this period I went to see Degas several times. He had grippe and was in a state of wild excitement, bouncing around in his bed. "I shall write a pamphlet," he said. "I shall start it

---

pictures to the State on condition that they should ultimately hang in the Louvre. When he died in 1893 the announcement of his bequest of sixty-five paintings caused violent discussion and discord. Politicians, academicians, and the majority of critics were all hostile to Impressionist painting. "For the government to accept such filth," said Gérôme, "would be the sign of a great moral decline."

Because of all the protests, and in spite of the provision in Caillebotte's will that the collection should enter the Luxembourg Museum undivided, Renoir, as executor of the will, was forced to compromise with the government lest the entire bequest be rejected. Of sixteen canvases by Monet, only eight were admitted; of eighteen by Pissarro, only seven; of eight by Renoir, six; of four by Manet, two; of five by Cézanne, two. Degas alone saw all seven of his works accepted.

71

with the sentence, 'This, too, is a bomb.' " That year anarchists were setting off bombs in Paris. The museum directors stood fast. They countered all criticism by stating their rights. Today no one gives all this a thought but I remember the affair vividly, and for me *The Pilgrims of Emmaüs* as it is now remains a painting that has been deflowered. Braun and Co. have old photographs showing the difference clearly.)

22 December 1895

Went to see Degas this morning. Is there better talk than I heard yesterday at Mme Darmesteter's[1] and today at Degas's? He was still in bed at quarter past nine and he said good morning in the way that he does only in bed where he seems like a child. Two very pretty Restoration portraits were standing on two armchairs. I looked at him and said, "What is this new acquisition?"

"Two Delacroix!" he said, all of a sudden awake and leaping out of bed. "And thereby hangs a tale. They come, if you can believe it, from the *pension* Goubaux, a boarding school that was still in existence in my time. This Goubaux was a teacher and writer; he founded the Collège Chaptal. But between 1821 and 1835 he had a *pension*. He hired Delacroix, who was very young then, to paint for his reception room portraits of the pupils who won prizes in their general examinations. May I present to you M. Bussy d'Hédouville, second-form scholar, second prize for Latin theme, and this other young man, second prize for Latin translation? Isn't destiny a strange thing? Here are two young idiots immortalized because they won prizes in the general examination! And look how pretty my portraits are — so cleverly, freely done. Delacroix did them like a great man who enjoys everything. Do you know Corot's remark?

1. Madame Darmesteter, née Mary Robinson, born in England, married in 1902 Emile Duclaux, director of the Pasteur Institute, who died in 1944, a refugee at Aurillac. I wrote a study of this distinguished woman entitled *Les Trois Mary* which was published as preface to *Mary Duclaux et Maurice Barrès: Lettres échangées*, Grasset, 1959. D.H.

Someone asked him how he had made so many beautiful things; he replied, 'Because I have never been bored.' "

While he was talking Degas dressed and while dressing he would take down from the wall or pick up from the floor a canvas or a woodcut to show me.

"Here is my new Van Gogh, and my Cézanne. I buy, I buy. I can't stop myself. The trying thing is that people are beginning to know it, so they bid against me. They know that when I want something I absolutely must have it. So they force me out on a limb. The other day that beast Chéramy bid against me. He hid behind the auctioneer's desk. I didn't see him but I was told he was there. I raised my bid five francs, then another five francs, then I was off. And when I got it there was my Chéramy coming out of his hiding place to stand beside me and say in his ham-actor voice, 'Delighted, *cher Maître,* that this masterpiece belongs to you.' I said to him, 'Delighted, delighted, that's all very well! You made me pay a high price for it and you didn't get it. Nine hundred francs is an enormous price for me to pay.' "

"Nine hundred francs for this portrait by Delacroix. But that's nothing. Are Delacroix as cheap as that?"

"Yes," said Degas, enraptured, his voice very low as if he were afraid of being overheard.

Then he sat down to breakfast. Zoé [Degas's maid] read the paper aloud and Degas kept interrupting with extraordinarily eloquent comments on the subject of France. We went out; he talked about France, about photography; about photography and about France, all mixed together with equal excitement. He took me to Glasset's, his photographer, and showed me his latest proofs — Mallarmé and Renoir, one of the Manet family, one of Madame Howland.

"Isn't it beautiful? But she won't see it. She'll let her dog lick it. She's a beast. The other day I showed her my beautiful Haas.[2] 'It's all mottled,' she said. 'You'll have to touch it up.'

2. "Charles Haas entered into the limelight in the most unpredictable way. For our Haas was Swann, the illustrious Swann. The astonishing graph of his life had amused and interested Proust. Doubtless he even envied it, and he made Haas the hero of his novel. . . .

Monster! I said nothing, gave her a look, did up my package and departed. The only woman one can photograph is your mother and she doesn't care."

"But she does care; only she's courageous."

"She does care?" He laughed. "But men are the same. They say, 'You haven't caught my expression.' " And he laughed some more. "As for me, I find that I always have too nice an expression."

"But you have a nice expression," I said.

"But I want to have a fierce one."

"Then you must make a face."

"But without making a face."

"Then you will have a very nice expression."

"You mean I am nice?" he exclaimed, laughing uproariously as he left me.

A Jew of obscure origin, Haas had early in life made it his aim to enter the most exclusive society and to spend his life there at a time when there really was an exclusive society. He formulated this plan around 1860. The slow, skillful, witty maneuvers that he then thought up were never recorded. They were later invented by the genius of Marcel Proust. I can remember having heard only admiration for the cleverness combined with luck that enabled him to force his way into the Jockey Club, the first and last of his race to cross that threshold: he had taken advantage of the Siege of Paris. Besides, to crown his success, Charles Haas found his poet: Marcel Proust.

"Haas behaved like a man of leisure, indeed pretended to be one. Actually his idleness was a mask to screen his ambition which created in him a constant anxiety that even showed in his wit, which was a little forced and tiresome. 'To go to Asnières, I would prefer Haas,' my father used to say, 'but to go to Constantinople I would choose Cavé.' And Degas: 'This Haas, how utterly contrived he is.' " Daniel Halévy, *Pays Parisiens.*

M. Halévy is not wholly fair to Haas, nor quite accurate. The "advantage" he took of the Siege of Paris, which won him membership in the Jockey Club, was marked bravery on the field of battle; and there has been a Rothschild in the Jockey Club.

My Friend Degas : Chapter II

I HAD INTENDED restricting the text of this book to excerpts copied from the notebooks I kept in my youth, but I am now forced to change my procedure. For at this time the circumstances of our personal lives changed. My brother and I had finished our courses at the university that kept us in Paris for months at a time. My parents had bought a place in the country where they stayed from early May through late October. On the other hand, my brother often lived in England and I spent months in Italy. Therefore we saw Degas less often, but our intimacy continued.

Degas's eyesight had grown steadily worse and the point had come when he could hardly see enough even to draw a few lines. He simplified his means of expression until no further simplification was possible. Depressed by the dark, the solitary artist gave up the solitude that had enabled him to produce so much work. When one of the sons of his friend Henri Rouart[1] decided to become a painter Degas asked him to work in his studio to keep him company. He still felt able to work a little, to give advice. Ernest Rouart could perhaps be helpful to him in handling

1.   Henri Rouart (1833–1912) was a metallurgical engineer and manufacturer of great wealth. He was also a discriminating art collector and a talented amateur painter who showed with the Impressionists. His son, Ernest, also a painter, married Julie Manet, the daughter of Berthe Morisot and Eugène Manet, brother of Edouard.

his paints and brushes. At Degas's suggestion young Rouart went to the Louvre where he studied the painters of the early Italian Renaissance by making copies. Degas, who as a young man had been passionately absorbed in them, no doubt derived a certain pleasure from watching his painstaking pupil experience the same excitement. There was one picture by Mantegna of which he had made a study in 1860 and which his young disciple in turn copied.[2]

But we mustn't overestimate the amount of satisfaction Degas could derive from guiding a young mind. It was a consolation to him, but it hardly satisfied his unfailing creative passion. None of his friends, I think, even suspected him of a poetic bent, but we knew very little of his past. The remarkable results he obtained make me think he was not wholly a novice in this field. In 1857, when Degas was in his twenties, there appeared the strange volume that brought Baudelaire into the courts. Although Degas never spoke of him, we must not infer that he ignored his work. Degas's mind was rich in secrets. In the verses that we shall see there is a Baudelairian precision. But without emphasizing any such assumption, the fact remains that we were not to listen to a novice; we were to hear a poet. The difficulties of writing, which he often confided to us, were a challenge worthy of Degas the artist. As a poet the elderly Degas was a child. This he knew and admitted.

At the time of which we are speaking, the world of poets was paying great honor to the Hispano-French poet José-Maria de Hérédia who wrote only sonnets. He produced very few. Indeed his whole work consisted of about one hundred, none of which he had then published. His admirers exercised all their ingenuity in getting hold of a manuscript and having it copied. The fortunate possessor of one of these copies in beautiful handwriting on fine paper cherished it as an ornament to his library.

2. In his youth Degas made an unfinished copy at the Louvre of Mantegna's *Christ Crucified between the Two Thieves*. He also wrote the axiom, "Try to combine Mantegna's spirit and love with Veronese's verve and color."

To me, to our little group of friends, Degas's first sonnet[3] came as a surprise. Dedicated to José-Maria de Hérédia, it came out of the blue and was recited with the great care that every poet attaches to his own work. It began thus:

> *Vous n'écorcherez pas un Marsyas de peu;*
> *Lourdement de jouer, un soir lui prit l'envie;*
> *Avant de regagner son ordinaire vie,*
> *Il baise et vous remet l'outil sacré du jeu.*

Degas never tired of repeating the last lines with a singing inflection in his voice:

> *Vous entonnez alors, orgeuil et vermeil*
> *Le rude chant qui plaît à l'Histoire, couchée*
> *Sur vos genoux, après des courses au soleil.*

On learning that Degas was becoming a poet, Berthe Morisot smiled: "And those women in their tubs? What will he do with them?"

The new young poet willingly admitted the difficulties he encountered in his work. He stopped Mallarmé in the street to complain of his troubles. "It isn't that I lack ideas," he said. "They come in waves, but to turn them into sonnets — how painful that is."

"Degas," the poet replied, "you don't make sonnets with ideas. You make them with words." Degas, become a pupil, repeated Mallarmé's lesson with delight.

The sonnet usually called the second, dedicated to Miss Mary Cassatt, has a striking title: *Perroquet.* Miss Cassatt was an old friend. Even before 1880 this great painter of women and children worked in Degas's studio, learning to strengthen her line-drawing. We assumed that they were close friends, but

3. The only edition of the sonnets is the excellent one published by M. Nepveu-Degas. The sonnet I have placed first is not first in his edition, but Degas never placed them in any order. For me, the sonnet humbly dedicated to José-Maria de Hérédia is the first of the series, the initial exercise in which the painter Degas shows that he is a poet when he wants to be. D.H.

never did I hear the sonnet dedicated to her read aloud to an amused audience. Never did I hear Miss Cassatt's name on Degas's lips.[4] During the severe winter of 1917 it was Miss Cassatt who informed the family that the presence of a woman was necessary at the bedside of the dying painter. Doubtless she was at the Montmartre cemetery on that last day; we did not greet her; very few of us knew her. I did not.

4. Degas did, however, mention Miss Cassatt in letters to a number of his friends between 1879 and 1890. In 1879 he acted as protective intermediary in the sale of one of her pictures, telling his correspondent that if the price quoted were satisfactory the buyer should deal directly with Miss Cassatt, if unsatisfactory Degas himself would take charge. To Pissarro he wrote in 1880, "Mademoiselle Cassatt is making some delightful experiments in engraving." And in the same year he expressed some anxiety over her having taken what seemed to him an unhealthy ground-floor studio, adding that the work she had done in the country that summer was "much firmer and nobler than what she did last year."

That the two painters corresponded we learn in a letter from Degas to Bartholomé in 1888: ". . . In reply to a letter of mine Mlle Cassat [sic] told me among other things that while she was riding in the forest her mare shied. She thought she saw some wild creatures moving in the grass, and when she reached home she saw that the horse's leg was swollen. It had been stung by a viper. It seems that viper-sting is less harmful to animals than to human beings, and doesn't kill them."

Degas's most personal feelings about Miss Cassatt are revealed in a letter to the Comte Lepic, often a model for Degas, a painter and engraver in his own right as well as a breeder of dogs. In a postscript to a request for a bitch to give to a friend Degas writes, "I think it only right that I should inform you that the person who wants this dog is Mlle Cassat [sic], that she has turned to me in this matter because I am known for the quality of my dogs and my affection for them, similar to my affection for old friends, etc., etc. I don't think it is necessary for me to give you any information about her. You know she is a good painter, devoting herself particularly just now to studies of light and shade on flesh and on dresses for which she has great feeling and skill . . .

"This distinguished person, by whose friendship I am as honored as you would be in my place, has asked me to be sure that you send her a young dog, young enough to love her." *Lettres de Degas.*

The "distinguished person's" feelings about her friend and men-

.   .   .   .

> *C'est vous qui le plaignez, non pas lui qui vous plaint;*
> *Le vôtre ... Mais sachez, comme un tout petit saint,*
> *Qu'un Coco se recueille et débite en sa fuite*
> *Ce qu'a dit votre coeur, au confident ouvert,*
> *Avec le bout de l'aile, enlevez-lui de suite*
> *Un bout de langue, alors il est muet ... et vert.*

Here the interplay of the words takes on a Mallarméan grace; the great poet's advice had not been ignored.

A third sonnet is dedicated to thoroughbreds. In the human category, there is the ballet dancer; in the animal, the racehorse. What innumerable studies he made of them; what pains he took.

Pur Sang

> *On l'entend approcher par saccade brisée,*
> *Le souffle fort et sain. Dès l'aurore venu,*
> *Dans le sévère train par son lad maintenu,*
> *Le bon poulain galope et coupe la rosée.*

---

tor are suggested in a conversation recorded in the *Memoirs* of the great collector, Mrs. Louisine Havemeyer. " '*Bon diseur de mots, mauvais caractère,*' " said Miss Cassatt. ... " 'Oh, my dear, he is dreadful! He dissolves your will.' " How could she get on with him, Mrs. Havemeyer wished to know. " 'Oh,' she answered, 'I am independent! I can live alone and I love to work. Sometimes it made him furious that he could find no chink in my armor, and there would be months when we just could not see each other. And then something I painted would bring us together and he would go to Durand-Ruel's and say something nice about me, or come to see me himself. When he saw my *Boy before the Mirror* he said to Durand-Ruel, " 'Where is she? I must see her at once. It is the greatest picture of the century." When I saw him he went over all the details of the picture with me and expressed great admiration for it, and then, as if regretting what he had said, added relentlessly, "It has all your qualities and all your faults — *c'est l'Enfant Jesus et sa bonne anglaise.*" ... But,' continued Miss Cassatt after a quiet moment, and I saw her face light up with a beautiful expression, 'magnificent! And however dreadful he was, he always lived up to his ideals. ... He is a philosopher, and there it is,' she said." Louisine Havemeyer, *Sixteen to Sixty: Memoirs of a Collector,* New York, 1961.

On the next page the dance and the dancer are his subject.

Il semble qu'autrefois la nature indolente,
Sûre de la beauté de son repos dormait,
Trop lourde, si toujours la grâce ne venait
L'éveiller de sa voix heureuse et haletante.

Mademoiselle Sanlaville, the subject of another sonnet, taught dancing at the Opéra and gave indispensable advice on every new ballet produced in her time.

Tout ce que le beau mot pantomime dit
Et tout ce que la langue agile, mensongère,
Du ballet dit à ceux qui percent le mystère
Des mouvements d'un corps éloquent et sans bruit.

Qui s'entêtent à voir en la femme qui fuit,
Incessante, fardée, arlequine, sévère,
Glisser la trace de leur âme passagère,
Plus vive qu'une page admirable qu'on lit,

Tout, et le dessin plein de la grâce savante,
Une danseuse l'a, lasse comme Atalante:
Tradition sereine, impénétrable aux fous.

Sous le bois méconnu, votre art infini veille:
Par le doute ou l'oubli d'un pas, je songe à vous,
Et vous venez tirer d'un vieux faune l'oreille.

The last sonnet I shall mention is dedicated to Rose Caron, the Brunehilde in *Sigurd*.[5] I think that Degas, the artist, loved better than anything tragedy illuminated by all the resources of song and of the dance. But his enjoyment of opera was strictly limited. Perhaps he experienced it only when Rose Caron of the

5. Rose Caron (1853–1930) enchanted Degas who went repeatedly to hear her sing Brunehilde in Ernest Reyer's opera *Sigurd*. Degas mentions her several times in his letters: ". . . I am the bear who habitually sucks the honey of *Sigurd* which I have seen again. . . . Divine Mme Caron — while talking to her I compared her to Puvis de Chavannes's figures. She didn't know them." And in another letter, "Mme Caron's arms are still there. She knows so well how long to keep them raised, with no affectation, just those divine, slender arms, a long time in the air, then gently lowered." Degas made a sketch of Mme Caron with her arms outstretched.

Series of scenes for a charade.
Posed but not photographed by Degas.

Madame Howland.
Photograph by Degas.

Courtesy of Madame Joxe.

Paris Opéra sang the role of Elizabeth in *Tannhaüser* or of Wagner's Brunehilde.

The two final tercets of this sonnet are very moving.

> *Après avoir jeté sa menace parée,*
> *Cette voix qui venait, divine de durée,*
> *Prendre Sigurd ainsi que son destin voulait.*
>
> *Tout ce beau va me suivre encore un bout de vie ...*
> *Si mes yeux se perdaient, que me durât l'ouïe,*
> *Au son, je pourrais voir le geste qu'elle fait.*

During the few weeks that Degas was writing these lines he recited them to his friends with childlike pleasure. But the sonnet dedicated to Rose Caron was exempt from all banter.

THERE WAS a time when Degas seemed to be uniquely preoccupied, even obsessed by the drafting of these sonnets. Whether this meant that during that period he abandoned painting there is no way of knowing, for he never kept a record of his work. But I am inclined to think that this was a sterile time for the painter. The difficulties that Degas was now encountering in his painting would year by year become impossibilities. Otherwise he could never have found the freshness of inspiration that charmed us in his sonnets, the same freshness that was to charm us in some of his photographs. For he now took up this new occupation. He acquired a camera and used it with the same energy that he put into everything. Aided by the daylight, and even by lamplight he wanted to resume his life-work — to play with light and shadow. He was ablaze with enthusiasm and all his friends were requisitioned. He appropriated their living-rooms. Here is a description of an evening that I wrote in my journal.

29 December 1895

Last night we had a charming dinner party: Uncle Jules, Henriette, Aunt Niaudet and her two daughters, and Degas. Uncle Jules talks very little, my aunt not at all. So that left the conversation to us, to the three young girls, and to Degas. These girls are charming, particularly Henriette — so delicate, so pale, so small, like the heroine of an English novel.

Uncle Jules is a very old friend of Degas, but he rarely sees him except at our house as they live so far apart. We were sure that Degas would be very glad to see Henriette. He is so affectionate. About two years ago when he was in Touraine he lunched at Montguerre with the Taschereau-Niaudets. He told Mama about this luncheon. "They must have found me very odd," he said, "but you wouldn't believe, Louise, how much it moved me to find myself there with those grown-up children. I couldn't think of a thing to say to them." Mama has often thought of inviting them together, but she was afraid of how Degas's rather bawdy words might sound to these very old-fashioned young girls. However, since they are all now in their twenties, Mama decided to invite them.

I sat between Henriette on my right and Mathilde on my left, and Degas to the left of Mathilde.

It bores me to repeat what was said. Degas was gay, obviously happy. He leaned towards his neighbor and talked to her graciously. After dinner he went to his studio with Uncle Jules to fetch his camera. A fortnight ago Degas dined with us, with Uncle Jules, too, and the Blanches. After dinner he went to fetch his camera and I went with him. He talked all the time. In his studio I noticed a variety of little pictures from his youth, showing his sister and his brothers. He had been looking for them. After we returned he happened to say to Uncle Jules — I don't know how — "It would have upset me to go alone, but Daniel kept me company." The sadness of this remark struck me; and it certainly struck my uncle. Because yesterday when Degas left alone, my uncle got up and went with him.

They returned together and from then on the *pleasure* part of the evening was over. Degas raised his voice, became dictatorial, gave orders that a lamp be brought into the little salon and that anyone who wasn't going to pose should leave. The *duty* part of the evening began. We had to obey Degas's fierce will, his artist's ferocity. At the moment all his friends speak of him with terror. If you invite him for the evening you know what to expect: two hours of military obedience.

In spite of my orders to leave, I slid into a corner and silent in the dark I watched Degas. He had seated Uncle Jules, Mathilde, and Henriette on the little sofa in front of the piano. He went back and forth in front of them running from one side of the room to the other with an expression of infinite happiness. He moved lamps, changed the reflectors, tried to light the legs by putting a lamp on the floor — to light Uncle Jules's legs, those famous legs, the slenderest, most supple legs in Paris which Degas always mentions ecstatically.

"Taschereau," he said, "hold onto that leg with your right arm, and pull it in there, there. Then look at that young person beside you. More affectionately — still more — come — come! You can smile so nicely when you want to. And you, Mademoiselle Henriette, bend your head — more — still more. Really bend it. Rest it on your neighbor's shoulder." And when she didn't follow his orders to suit him he caught her by the nape of the neck and posed her as he wished. He seized hold of Mathilde and turned her face towards her uncle. Then he stepped back and exclaimed happily, "That does it."

The pose was held for two minutes — and then repeated. We shall see the photographs tonight or tomorrow morning, I think. He will display them here looking happy — and really at moments like that he is happy.

At half-past eleven everybody left; Degas surrounded by three laughing girls carried his camera, as proud as a child carrying a gun.

(Degas made other attempts by himself, the kind of adventures to which he would not have exposed anyone else. He reported joyfully on one moonlight night when he had gone out alone with his camera: "A group of people collected near me," he said. "I heard the murmur of their voices. They probably thought I was crazy." But the outcome of these nocturnal efforts we never knew. Degas did not reveal the results of his experiments.)

This morning at Degas's. We talked about the Transvaal: seven hundred English have invaded the Boer States. We talked about the English and I talked of the religiosity of the Boers, at least as much as I know about it. He listened with interest and then said, "How pleasant it is to think that there are such odd people in the world." And I added, "And that there are more of them coming along every day. The Boers are yesterday's." Whereupon a great explosion from Degas.

"Let us hope that we shall soon have finished with art, with aesthetics. They make me sick. Yesterday I dined at the Rouarts'. There were his sons and some young people — all talking art. I blew up. What interests me is work, business, the army!"

Degas this morning having made three or four brief remarks that are difficult to report, I shall make a resumé of what I have heard him say about hyperaesthesia, the aesthetic hypertrophy of our contemporaries.

I believe that his revolt originated with the opening of Liberty's shop in Paris. He went with his friend Bartholomé and said to him, "So much taste will lead to prison." This remark he repeated last year to Oscar Wilde. He saw Wilde at Aunt Geneviève's where they had a long, brilliant conversation. For example:

Wilde: "You know how well known you are in England —"
Degas: "Fortunately less so than you."[6]

All the attempts at artistic furnishing in the last few years exasperate him. At the Champ de Mars exhibition he was hailed

6. Oscar Wilde's opinion of Degas is expressed in an 1894 letter to W. E. Henley who wanted to get a statement from Degas for publication in the *National Observer*. "You asked me about Degas. Well, he loves to be thought young, so I don't think he would tell his age. He disbelieves in art-education, so I don't think he will name a Master. He despises what he cannot get, so I am sure he will not give any information about prizes or honours. Why say anything about his person? His pastels are himself." *The Letters of Oscar Wilde.*

by Montesquiou[7] who was standing guard in front of an apple-green bed he had designed with Sallé. Degas delivered a great speech in front of about a hundred people. Unfortunately I have forgotten some of it.

"Do you think," he said, "that you will conceive better children in an apple-green bed? Watch out, M. de Montesquiou; taste is a vice." And he turned his back on Montesquiou — whose reputation is not too good — this was after the Oscar Wilde affair.

Pederasty and taste — Degas makes no distinction between them. It seems that a "Maison de l'Art Nouveau" has recently opened in which young women sell objects in good taste. Degas said, "It is a good thing they used women clerks; if they had had men the police would already have closed the place."

He stamped his foot this morning in the rue Mansard: "Taste! It doesn't exist. An artist makes beautiful things without being aware of it. Aesthetes beat their brows and say to themselves, 'How can I find a pretty shape for a chamberpot?' Poor creatures, their chamberpots may be works of art but they will immediately induce a retention of urine! They will look at their pots and say to all their friends: 'Look at my chamberpot. Isn't it pretty?' No more art! No more art! No more art!"

21 January 1896

Degas. The Ingres are bought. I went to his house this morning to spend ten minutes hearing about them. He insisted on

7. Comte Robert de Montesquiou-Fezensac (1855–1921), descended from the earliest Kings of France, from d'Artagnan the musketeer, was a living embodiment of French history whose pride of race was second only to his literary ambition. The author of *Hortensias bleus* and many other volumes of poetry, he was inordinately vain. He had himself photographed over two hundred times and painted by Whistler, Helleu, Boldini and others. In his own day he was famed for his taste and the elaborate fêtes which he set against the decor of the series of elaborate "pavilions" and apartments he inhabited. Today his fame rests largely on his having been the model for Marcel Proust's Baron de Charlus.

keeping me there for three hours. We strolled along the rue Lafitte announcing the victory to the dealers.

In the evening he came to the house and said, "I have come because I feel like talking." Again the tale of the purchase.

"I shall die in a poorhouse but that's a fine thing." Rather a disconcerting remark.

"Yes, I shall give the Ingres portraits to my country; and then I shall go and sit in front of them and look at them and think about what a noble deed I have done."

31 January 1896

At dinner: the John Lemoinnes, Jacques Blanche, and Degas . . . who is still stupefied with happiness over his two Ingres portraits.

After Jacques and his ladies left, Degas stayed a little while, talking about his picture gallery, his difficulties with Zoé who demands blue aprons because her master buys Ingres. Roaring with laughter he tells us of his quarrels with her. And still laughing he leans back in his chair and suddenly he says: "To have no clothes and to own sublime objects — that will be my *chic!*"

18 November 1896

I was on my way to the Berthelots'.[8] That very morning they

8. The Berthelots were Daniel Halévy's first cousins. They were one of the most notable families of the Third Republic. The father, Marcelin, a distinguished chemist, occupied a number of important positions in the government and was a member of the Academy. His son Daniel, also a scientist, worked with the Curies. René, a philosopher, was professor at the University of Brussels. Philippe, after entering the Foreign Service at an early age, became in 1920 Permanent Secretary for Foreign Affairs. The most brilliant, interesting, and least known son was André who, after compiling a remarkable Encyclopedia of human knowledge with the aid of his brothers, traveled throughout Africa and China where he founded the *Banque de Chine*. Later he designed, financed, and administered the Paris Metro.

"I often went to the Institute where my Berthelot cousins lived . . ." wrote M. Halévy. "From the dark entry you proceeded through a hall, brushing against book-cases loaded with folio volumes. Off this

had lost Hélène, who died in childbirth. As I went into the rue Lafitte, I saw Degas who passed right by me. He was only a step or two away but didn't see me. Walking with head bowed, wrapped from top to toe in his Inverness cape, he looked like a phantom at dusk. I stopped him. He was coming from the Jeanniot exhibition at Durand-Ruel's. He spoke a few words, and I interrupted him to say, "I am going to the Berthelots'; their daughter is dead." "Oh," said Degas, raising his arms in a gesture of despair, then letting them fall. "Poor Sophie! If you see her give her my sympathy. Poor Sophie! I would like to write to her — but no, it would be too painful: 'To each of us . . .' Oh Lord, the whole world is dying around us." And he left.

Later, at home, the doorbell rang and I heard Degas's heavy steps in the dining-room. Then he came into the little sitting-room. He said a few words to Mother about Hélène's death. He opened a big envelope he was carrying under his arm and showed us the enlargements he had made with me the night before. There were photographs of Haas, of Reyer, of Du Lau, of Mme Howland. He looked at them, talked about the details with childlike joy. Then I read him an *Arabian Nights* tale and afterwards we talked a little. Suddenly he became depressed again as he almost always does these days unless there is some kind of artificial stimulus. Mother spoke of the young Englishman, Williams, whom we used to see last winter. "He enjoyed you very much," she said to Degas. " 'I didn't know I was as diverting as I am.' Who wrote that line?"[9] he added, as though ashamed of such an admission.

Then he told us about his nephews in Buenos Aires, the children of his sister who had just died. He recited their letters to

---

hall were the rooms of André, Philippe, Daniel, and then René's, my contemporary, who was quieter than the others. I often saw Marcelin Berthelot, who among grown-ups had the reputation for harshness. I only know that he was exquisite with us children and I never saw anything frightening in his magnificent face, his immense brow, in the depths of his piercing, powerful glance, the look of an eagle in no way astonished by my ignorant gaze." Daniel Halévy, *Pays Parisiens.*

9. Molière, *Le Misanthrope,* II, 7. *"Je ne croyais pas être si plaisant que je suis."*

us so fondly. Then he talked about Haas, people in society, and was gay again. But suddenly he left.

17 December 1896

At dinner this evening Degas, Yoyo, Catherine, Gregh, Rivoire, La Salle, Jacques, Rouquès, later Dreyfus.[1] Our little corner of the table — Yoyo, Jacques, Gregh, Degas, and me — was very lively. Gregh prodded Degas who laughed and was finally forced to admit that if Bernhardt recited his sonnets on the stage of the Renaissance he would be shamefully pleased. "What extraordinary things you young people make me say!"

After dinner we chatted for a long time, surrounding Degas, who talked about Mallarmé, the dance, and then we read the Ponchon[2] of the day — dedicated to Sarah.

> *Toi dans la grâce imbibe*
> *Même le Monsieur Scribe,*
> *Et qui nous rend doux*
> *Le plus Bardoux.*

1. Yoyo was the nickname of Jacques-Emile Blanche's sister-in-law, Marie-John Lemoinne.

Fernand Gregh, Louis de la Salle and Robert Dreyfus had all been schoolmates of Daniel Halévy and Marcel Proust at the Lycée Cordorcet. Gregh, a minor poet and author of a biography of Victor Hugo, was a special protegé of Ludovic Halévy's who secured for him the Académie prize for his first book of poems, *La Maison de l'enfance,* and also an editorial position on the *Revue de Paris.* This position M. Gregh resigned in favor of another minor poet, André Rivoire, who would otherwise, because of poverty, have been forced to return to his home in the provinces. M. Gregh, in his eighties, was elected a member of the Académie Française after seventeen attempts.

Louis de la Salle, also a minor poet, was killed early in the first World War.

Robert Dreyfus, a journalist on the staff of the *Figaro,* wrote historical and literary essays.

All of these young men except Rivoire collaborated with Marcel Proust and Daniel Halévy on the little review *Le Banquet,* which was born and nourished in the salon of Daniel's "aunt," Madame Straus.

2. Raoul Ponchon (1848–1937) for nearly thirty years wrote what he called *"gazettes rimées"* for the *Courrier Français* and the *Journal.*

The conversation died down. Gregh went to the piano and sang parts of *Rheingold* and *Gotterdämmerung*. . . . Degas came up to the piano and picked out some scores of Gluck — *Helen and Paris, O del dolce ardor Cramato oggetto*. . . . After *Helen, Orpheus*. . . .

Degas sat, his eyes closed, his head swaying to the rhythm of the music. Occasionally he laughed and repeated the Italian words that sounded strange in Gregh's pronunciation. These unpracticed performances give the most pleasure musically. Everyone works at them.

(Note the music that was played: Wagner first, soon put aside. Then Gluck. That was Degas's taste. Romantic music had no charms for him. I remember one evening when a friend, a woman pianist, suggested playing a Beethoven sonata to him. Gently he dissuaded her. "When I hear a theme of Beethoven's I feel as though I were walking alone in a forest filled with all my troubles. Play us something else.")

8 January 1897

. . . The talk was about a book that had just appeared called *Mêlée de jeunes*. "Ah," cried Degas, "they are annoying, these young people. They want us to believe that we are old — that we are ill, have white hair, are no longer able to pay court to a dancer. What of it? There's more to life than that. We have the will to work, we are not old. We must always remember the remark that David[3] made one day: 'I don't know what's wrong with me — my hands let me down, I can't do anything. Yet my mind is active, I am full of ideas. — My eyes bother me, I no longer hear, but what's wrong with me? I don't understand.' Whereupon he sank into a chair and died. — But old, no! We are not old."

7 February 1897

Last Tuesday Degas was very brilliant and lively. I went there to read him Antonin Proust's recollections of Manet.

---

3. The painter, Louis David (1748–1825).

"Proust gives him an attitude that I don't like," he said. "Manet was ever so much nicer, ever so much simpler. But writers always have to make people pose. It is like those statues of soldiers that you see everywhere, stiff-legged, their arms raised high. They are not like that. A soldier is a serious-minded man. I would like to see them with hands clasped behind their backs, heads bent in meditation.

I remind him of Faidherbe, that soldier in spectacles, in whose memory a ridiculously heroic statue had just been erected at Saint-Quentin.

"Naturally. Just so . . . and Gouvion Saint-Cyr! Do you know about him? He didn't even have a uniform, always wore a frock coat even on horseback in the battlefield. It was he who saved the day at Eylau. That beast Oudinot lost everything. Fortunately he was shot, had to be carried off the field. Gouvion took command and started fighting again. At night he stayed in a convent and played the violin; that was his passion. He never bothered about the soldiers but they adored him. 'That fellow will get us out of trouble,' they would say. When he was named general of a division he had to have a uniform made. . . . Napoleon depended on him for everything. 'I know only two chiefs,' he said, 'myself for attack, Gouvion for defense.' "

He day-dreamed for a while and then exclaimed, "What times we live in! I went to that exhibition this afternoon. There was a catalogue and a preface to the catalogue. — In the old days they beat the drum outside the encampments; today they play the lyre in picture galleries. What poetic boredom!"

Ponchon, a day or two ago, wrote about the plague:

> Elle nous vient d'Asie,
> Comme la poésie
> Et autres saletés
> Opium, thé.

20 February 1897

Degas during the first half of dinner, slightly sleepy, grumbled about everything and kept repeating himself so much that

Gregh finally took him to task: "You abuse the right to be aggressive, Monsieur Degas."

"No, no, it's not that. But this art that is invading us exacerbates me. Such talk, such ——."

"But it has always been like that, Monsieur Degas. Only in the past we saw nothing but the works themselves. Now we see the means by which they are produced, the *cuisine* so to speak. And that is always rather low."

"Listen," said Degas, awakened by the attack. He thought for a moment, then: "At the end of antiquity, when all the deities, all the legends had grown a little stale there was a man who wanted to revive them. I mean Ovid. He redid all these fables in verse, and the result was a hothouse full of artificial flowers. And Ovid was sent among the Scythians there to bemoan his false flowers. Well, everything that's done today, everything that's thought is as as false as those flowers — without leaves, without stems, without roots. It's artificial."

"Monsieur Degas, Monsieur Degas," Gregh rejoined. "You are so right that one doesn't know how to reply to you; and besides you put things so prettily — "

"What I have just said is not pretty," Degas answered. "It is a thought."

"A thought not lacking in form," Rivoire added.

"What do you expect?" Degas continued. "I can't stand all this poetry, this sophistry, and these young men in long-tailed morning coats holding lilies in their hands while they talk to women. Look, when you talk to a woman you need both hands, don't you?" And gesturing towards the women who were listening, he concluded, "I wish I could express myself more freely."

There was a moment of silence and then he started a long, jerky discourse interrupted by our laughter. Sometimes he addressed Auguste who was passing the dishes at table and made him laugh, too.

23 February 1897

Last night I read to Degas the second part of Antonin Proust's recollections of Manet, pubished in the *Revue Blanche.*

91

I found him alone in his little dressing-room. That is where he eats.

"Oh, it's you!"

"I have brought you the Manet."

"Read it."

I opened the magazine. He saw a drawing, took out his magnifying glass, and looked at it. It was a *café-concert* singer.

"That Manet," he said. "As soon as I did dancers, he did them. He always imitated. Read on."

I read. I had been reading for some time when I came to a brief sentence about the *Déjeuner sur l'herbe* and *plein air*. Degas stopped me.

"That's not true. He confuses everything. Manet wasn't thinking about *plein air* when he painted the *Déjeuner sur l'herbe*. He didn't think about it until he saw Monet's first paintings. He could never do anything but imitate.[4] Proust confuses the whole thing. Oh, literary people! Always meddling! *We do ourselves justice so adequately*. Read some more."

4. The friendship between Degas and Manet which started when they were both in their thirties was real but thorny. Temperamentally they were at opposite poles, Manet being as gregarious, as fond of pretty women, as eager for recognition as Degas was unsociable and indifferent to public esteem. But they were closer friends of each other than of any members of the Impressionist group with the exception of Berthe Morisot. They greatly admired each other's work but Degas would never give Manet the praise he so much needed to fortify him against the derision and scorn of the public which he bore throughout his life. Yet he would praise Manet to others, writing for instance to the painter Tissot, "I have seen a new thing of Manet's, medium-sized, so finished, so lovingly painted, a change, in fact. What a talented fellow he is!"

They quarreled a number of times (cf. p. 121), once when Manet cut Madame Manet's likeness off a portrait Degas had made of him and his wife, because he thought Degas had not done her justice. But the quarrels were always made up. And although in 1882 when Manet's last work, the *Bar aux Folies-Bergères*, was shown at the Salon, Degas wrote, "The Manet, both stupid and clever, a playing card with no depth, Spanish *trompe-l'oeil*," a year later on leaving Manet's funeral services he remarked, "We never knew how great he was."

I continued reading, and he interrupted from time to time with little technical corrections. I finished. "That's all," I said.

Degas was silent for a moment. He leaned back in his chair, looked around him, and then, in the beautiful, sad, intimate voice that I love, not in the combative one which has now become almost like a challenge to a duel, he said, "Oh, the critics! They won't leave you in peace. What a fate! To be handed over to writers!"

During the day I had been to see Degas's pictures shown at the Luxembourg. "Would it make you unhappy," I asked him, "if I talked to you about your pictures at the Luxembourg?"

"Not at all. Go ahead."

"You told me this morning that you were dissatisfied with them, that the selection wasn't representative. I don't agree with you. Granted there are none of your large pictures. But you can't expect small pictures to be anything but small pictures, and the ones that are there are really as perfect, as beautiful, as small pastels can be."

"It's a long time since I've seen them. Perhaps I would like them better than I think. But I haven't any very clear idea of them."

"The specially good thing is the great variety. Your whole work is very successfully represented. There is the dancer tying her slipper which is simply a drawing, an admirable drawing. There are the women in front of a café — "

"Yes, a café on the boulevard with the crowd going by in the background."

"That one rather on the cruel, cynical side. Beside it is that ballerina dancing all alone — grace and poetry embodied."

"I did lots of women like that. And the chorus of *Don Juan,* too. All of them are more or less rapid sketches. If you have to go to the Luxembourg, it is annoying to go in such impromptu style. I haven't been there. I don't know whether I have the courage to go. Yesterday I went to Boutet de Monvel's, that nice boy — right next door. The museum was closed, but even if it had been open I don't know whether I could have gone in. I was told that there were lots of people. Is that so? Why, why, good Lord, should there be so many people? Can't they leave you alone? No. They regiment you; they grab hold of you. People say to me: 'At last, you are there!' Where? Where am I? They are the people who, when they were starting their careers, dreamed of occupying Bouguereau's place. 'You are there!' Shouldn't we have been there forty years ago? They bought all the second-class medals. 'At last!' I am told that I should be happy and profit by all this. That's not my way of thinking. I want to succeed where I want, when I want, and how I want. My God! People crowding around our pictures, why? Do they crowd into a chemist's laboratory? You have read how Manet used a black mirror to gauge values. All that is very complicated. What can they understand about it? Nothing! A chemist works in peace. We, we belong to everybody! What anguish!" After a rather long silence he added, "All this deprives me of the prestige that was so lovely." Then he went on with great violence:

"Théodore Duret,[5] that Duret who is mentioned in the memoirs you have just been reading, what a man! He had pictures by all of us. He sold them two years ago, and he himself solemnly wrote the preface to his own catalogue. 'I was their friend. I frequented their studios. Therefore I can be relied upon when I say that what I am selling today is the best of their work.' I went to his exhibition. He was there. He tried to shake hands with me. I refused. He said: 'What are you thinking of? Us, two old friends? I can send you my seconds.' 'You can send me what you like,' I said, 'but I won't shake hands with you. If you are bankrupt, if you have to sell your pictures, you should at least sell them sadly. But you glorify yourself as having been one of our friends. You have pasted up signs all over Paris: *Duret Sale*. I won't shake hands with you. Besides, your auction will fail. Some of us are well represented in your collection, others not. You are losing our respect and you won't make any money.'

5. Théodore Duret (1838–1927), journalist and art critic, was one of the early champions of Manet and the Impressionists. Among his writings were a biography of Manet, who painted his portrait, and a history of the Impressionist movement.

It was a terrible execution. He turned pale and so did I." Again silence.

"I am not a misanthrope, far from it. But it is sad to go on living surrounded by swine. Tissot,[6] that old friend I lived with so long, had such fun with, knew so well, and who bought several of my pictures. He sold them; that was his affair. But the other day when I went into Durand-Ruel's I said, 'How do you happen to have that?' 'It's Tissot's,' he said. 'I gave it to him.' 'He sold it to me,' Durand-Ruel replied.

"I was about to write Tissot a terrible letter. But what's the use? I shall do up some drawings he once gave me and send them back to him without a word. He'll understand. For him to have sold it! Now he's got religion. He says he experiences inconceivable joy in his faith. At the same time he not only sells his own products high but sells his friends' pictures as well. — Practically everyone I have given pictures to has sold them. . . . To think that we lived together as friends and then — Well, I can take my vengeance. I shall do a caricature of Tissot with Christ behind him, whipping him, and call it: *Christ Driving his Merchant from the Temple.* My God!"

We went out. In order to distract him a little I said, "Is it true that you wanted to marry my cousin Henriette?"

"You know about that?" He burst into laughter. "She is

6. James Tissot (1836–1902), a pupil of Ingres, whose magnificent portrait by Degas hangs in the Metropolitan Museum, was an habitué of the cafés and the boulevards during the sixties when he painted a series of studies that he called *La Femme à Paris.* He fought in the Franco-Prussian war, but according to Jacques-Emile Blanche, he was afraid that when the Commune came into power his house might be destroyed by the Federal troops, so he became briefly a Communard. Although this act was never held against him by the government, he emigrated to England where he stayed for a number of years before returning to France. There he had a beautiful mysterious mistress who frequently served as his model but whom his friends never saw. When she died, Tissot turned to religion. After a visit to Palestine he made some seven hundred watercolor drawings to illustrate the Bible for which he was paid 1,100,000 francs. Three hundred and fifty drawings of incidents in the life of Christ were shown in Paris in 1895.

nice, isn't she? Sweet — very nice. I approached her father. He said, 'Ask her yourself.' So when I was helping her into a cab I said, 'Mademoiselle Henriette, your father has given me permission to ask for your hand.' So, instinctively, she gave me her hand. 'But no.' I cried, 'I want to marry you.' I told her that if she wanted me to dye my hair I would. It was all because of that fool of a Zoé whom I had fired that morning. I said to her, 'You make me regret that I am not married. How can a man live with an idiot, a fool like you?' I had not yet told her that I was going to be married. When I have a wife, Zoé will have to toe the mark . . ." He was still laughing aloud when he boarded the streetcar.

Degas, Ludovic Halévy, and Cavé in 1885.
Photograph by Barnes, Dieppe.
Courtesy of Bibliothèque Nationale.

Degas c. 1885, with the Lemoinne sisters,
Elie and Daniel Halévy, posed by Degas as a
parody of Ingres' *Apotheosis of Homer*.
Photograph by Barnes, Dieppe.

Courtesy of Bibliothèque Nationale.

My Friend Degas : Chapter III

AN ALMOST unbelievable thing happened in the autumn of 1897. Our long-standing friendship with Degas, which on our mother's side went back to their childhood, was broken off. Nothing in our past relationship indicated that politics could cause such a break. Degas never seemed to have any political opinions. Painting was his work, and his work was his entire life. But I think I can see the devious way by which the anxieties of public life invaded his being. I can't pretend that my explanation will not appear paradoxical. But you must not forget that in dealing with Degas you are dealing with a profoundly paradoxical man. Even in his art you can see this. An example of his paradoxical taste during his fifties was the reading of serialized romances, especially the historical novels of Dumas. Zoé, his maid, read them aloud to him during meals. He listened quite uncritically. After the increasing difficulties in the studio these solitary meals were restful. The elder Dumas was admirably suited to distract the unquestioning mind. Degas listened, docile, happy. The history of France according to Dumas was a source of romantic emotion. But Degas happened to change authors.

In 1892 the newspaper *La Libre Parole,* edited by Edouard Drumont,[1] began to appear, and the children of his friend Henri Rouart were enamored of it. For a decade there had been serious

1. Edouard Drumont (1844–1917), author of *La France Juive* (1886), was the chief exponent of anti-Semitism in France.

scandals that seemed to indicate a debasing of French morality and this had worried Degas. Drumont, a powerful pamphleteer, offered an explanation of this decline, and Degas listened to his daily article as docilely as he had listened to the tales of Dumas *père*. He soon became a passionate reader of Drumont, but because of my father's Jewish origin he was always very careful not to show us his own intense anti-Semitism. With me he expressed his opinions freely, but I never thought that our friendship would one day be broken by them. Nevertheless that is what happened. The following entry in my journal is dated

12 November 1897
Last night we dined with Degas.

Degas in his new residence; three stories: sleep on the second, eat on the third, work on the fourth, the *concierge* explained. On the second the picture-gallery, on the third his own old sketches and drawings, on the fourth the studio.

Dinner not very brilliant, rather a family affair.

Nor am I very brilliant at the moment. Entirely incapable of writing, and yet everything to do with Degas is picturesque — more than that: really great. What a man!

REREADING these lines written so long ago, I suspect that if the dinner-table conversation remained mediocre it was because each one of us was tormented by our preoccupation with thoughts we had to suppress. The significance of the Dreyfus Affair, still an obscure threat to most of the country, was entirely clear to us because my brother was a student at the Ecole Normale in the rue d'Ulm, which to the end was one of the leading centers of the pro-Dreyfus campaign. The librarian there was Lucien Herr[2] who knew everything there was to know about the affair and whose name will go down in history. Through him we knew that Esterhazy was the real traitor, and

2. Lucien Herr (1864–1926), the moving force in fomenting the movement for the retrial of Captain Dreyfus, was also librarian of the Ecole Normale Supérieure, a member of the staff of the *Revue de Paris* and mentor and inspirer of the great Socialist, Jean Jaurès.

also the name of the General Staff officer, Lieutenant-Colonel Picquart, who had in vain revealed the truth to his superiors in an effort to make them see that a full exposure of the Dreyfus Affair was a national necessity. Indeed the German General Staff knew the truth as well as we did, and at any moment it was possible for them to rouse French public opinion by publishing the staggering facts. If the official publication of the facts were immediate and frank, the shock could be rapidly overcome. But the chiefs of the General Staff had not only refused to listen to Colonel Picquart; they had ousted him from France and appointed him commander of a regiment in a dangerous zone of the Tunisian Sahara. This we knew from Lucien Herr. Did the novelist Alexandre Dumas *père* ever invent a more bewildering episode?

I find the following entry in my journal for

14 November 1897

Our usual Thursday dinner — Anatole France, Lemaître, Degas, and Reyer. (Actually an unusual dinner table where we were hosts to Anatole France and Jules Lemaître, intimate friends and the two masters of the kind of skepticism they called Renanism. Shortly after this evening they were separated by an abyss. France became the chief of anti-military Dreyfusism, and Lemaître headed the new militarism against the revision of the Dreyfus trial.)

Rather brilliant conversation but I'm unable to report it because my mind wandered. Where was I?

This Dreyfus Affair has come violently into my life. I am sure now of my political opinions. I am very republican, very individualistic; I hate demagogy which is against liberty. When I was young I was a Boulangist; it was so gay, so brilliant! I am ashamed of it today. Yet Boulangism and the Dreyfus Affair are alike; clericalism and demagogy; popular incitement legalized.

C'est ici le combat du jour et de la nuit!

I have been thinking these last few days of that line of Hugo's. I felt while reading the *Libre Parole,* the *Intransigeant,* the *Patrie,* a dark abyss opening to engulf us: mob instincts, the masses. The masses have always been the enemy of society. The aristocratic solution is to conquer them. The democratic (detestable word) is to suppress them while transforming them.

22 November 1897

Yesterday evening before dinner I was playing the piano when Papa half-opened the door. "I am late," he said, "but I have tales to tell. Come along."

I followed him. He came from the *Revue de Paris*. There Herr had given him the most surprising news. He is an intimate friend of Demange and knows a lot. When Scheurer-Kestner went to find Billot,[3] he put the dossier on his table.

"Here. Here is the proof of Dreyfus's innocence."

"Dreyfus's innocence!" Billot exclaimed. "Why, I have known about it for a year and a half."

Mama and I were sitting in front of Papa when he spoke these words — and although we had both been convinced for a long time that the government knew, we were shocked and said nothing. . . .

Thursday, 25 November 1897

Last night, chatting among ourselves at the end of the evening — until then the subject had been proscribed as Papa was on edge, Degas very anti-Semitic — we had a few moments of delightful gaiety and relaxation.

IT WAS the last of our happy conversations. Our friendship was to end suddenly and in silence; but it perished without any re-

3. Edgar Demange (1841–1925), a devout Catholic and distinguished lawyer, known for a long series of brilliant defenses in criminal cases, undertook the defense of Dreyfus in 1894 and again in 1899.

Auguste Scheurer-Kestner (1833–1899), a close friend and associate of Gambetta and vice-president of the Senate, became convinced in 1895 of Dreyfus's innocence and worked unceasingly for a retrial.

General Jean-Baptiste Billot (1827–1907), Minister of War 1896 to 1898, played a large part in the rebuilding of the French army after the defeat of 1870. To prevent the retrial he used all means at his disposal, including the arrest of Colonel Picquart.

grettable exchange of words. One last time Degas dined with us. Who the other guests were I don't remember. Doubtless young people who didn't care what they said. Degas remained silent. Conscious of the threat that hung over us, I watched his face attentively. His lips were closed; he looked upwards almost constantly as though cutting himself off from the company that surrounded him. Had he spoken it would no doubt have been in defense of the army, the army whose traditions and virtues he held so high, and which was now being insulted by our intellectual theorizing. Not a word came from those closed lips, and at the end of dinner Degas disappeared.

The next morning my mother read without comment a letter addressed to her and, hesitating to accept its significance, she handed it in silence to my brother Elie. My brother said, "It is the language of exasperation." If my mother had asked me, I hope that I would have had enough composure to say, "I can understand Degas; he knows that our disagreement is so profound that we can only separate in dignified silence." ...

From then on the respect I retained for Degas was often tested. I remember a dinner at which he was execrated. I couldn't bear it and said that a man could not be judged by one simple opinion. But a hue and cry was raised against me, and I was so young that I would have found it difficult to face if I had not been backed by Renan's son, Ary, who had a very sharp tongue. "I have seen Degas's life for twenty years," he said, "and I have never known him to be at fault."

21 March 1898

This morning I went to see Degas whom I had not seen for three months. The Dreyfus Affair has interfered with our relationship; I haven't dared go back to see him.[4] He is so violent! But for the last few days I have known that he was ill. I waited

4. Daniel and Elie Halévy, Fernand Gregh, Anatole France, Claude Monet, Marcel Proust were among three thousand signers of the petition against the violation of procedure in the 1894 trial of Dreyfus which was drawn up shortly after Emile Zola's article *J'accuse* appeared in Clemenceau's paper *Aurore* on January 13, 1898.

until this morning in order to have a double pretext for my visit. Around nine o'clock he was still in bed.

"Oh, it's you?" he said and immediately greeted me with exquisite cordiality. Only his fine canine head emerged from under the sheets. He told me about his illness. I listened, then told him my news,[5] knowing that for several months he has no longer railed against marriage. "You understand now, don't you, that people do marry?"

"Oh, yes. I am alone. I see how happy Rouart's son is. It's a good thing to marry. — Ah, *la solitude* —"[6]

20 August 1899

Yesterday Rouart called. An old friend of my father and of Degas. Also an old friend of General Mercier.[7] Rouart is a graduate of the Polytechnic Institute, very much a soldier, but at the same time gentle and charming. His sons are fanatics. He is extremely moderate about the Affair. We talked about painting. He left, and I alone accompanied him. He told me that Degas sent me the most friendly greetings. I was very pleased and touched.

5. Daniel Halévy married Marianne Vaudoyer in November, 1898. Madame Halévy told me that one of the most painful experiences of her life had occurred as she started on her wedding journey. A girl of eighteen, she found her husband sitting beside her in a carriage, tears streaming down his face. "What have I done?" she asked. "It isn't you," he explained. "It's just . . . Degas didn't kiss you."

6. Degas said several times to the art dealer, Ambroise Vollard, "A man should marry. You don't know what the solitude of old age is like." "But why then have you never married, Monsieur Degas?" Vollard asked. "Oh, with me it's different. I was too afraid of hearing my wife say after I had finished a picture, 'That's a pretty thing you've done there.' " Ambroise Vollard, *Degas,* Paris, 1924.

7. General Auguste Mercier (1833–1921), Minister of War 1893 to 1895, was a little-known officer, unversed in politics. When at the end of his first year as minister he found himself in difficulties with the government and the army, he used the Dreyfus Affair to make his position secure.

My Friend Degas : Chapter IV

May 1904

I went to see Degas when someone told me that he had been ill with intestinal grippe for the last two months. I have let a long time go by without reporting that visit. Degas was at home; he had me brought to his studio. It gave me rather a shock to see him dressed like a tramp, grown so thin, another man entirely. He seemed touched and pleased to see me. He asked for news of all the family and then started right away talking compulsively.

"Education! What a crime! Look at the Bretons. As long as they make the sign of the cross they are good people. But take away their faith and they become cowards.[1] What a crime! Art for the people! How dreary! Beauty is a mystery —," and he repeated, "Beauty is a mystery." At one point he said, "Since our misfortunes."

He meant since the victory of the Dreyfusards. But I felt no embarrassment, no irritation. I listened to him with infinite respect as though he had been telling stories of another world; and he listened to me affectionately.

"Beauty is a mystery, but no one knows it any more. The recipes, the secrets are forgotten. A young man is set in the mid-

1. The separation of Church and State in France which took place officially in 1906 was under violent discussion at this time.

dle of a field and told, 'Paint.' And he paints a sincere farm. It's idiotic."

As I left he again asked me how everyone was at home.

1907

At the apartments of the Institute after the death of Marcelin Berthelot and his wife who died on the same day at the Institute, where they lived.

A day or two after their deaths as the two coffins were still there in the salon I went to the Institute with Marianne. Mama was there and René and Daniel and Camille.

"You know," René said, "Mama was interested in reading right up to the end. Clairin's recollections, his account of the death of Henri Regnault, she found touching. She remembered that Degas brought the news to your house, in the dining-room. He was overcome with emotion."

Henri Regnault,[2] son of the scholar, was a friend of both of ours; Degas, too. Singular, the relationships between notable families.

1908

Death of my father; visit from Degas.

I had been forewarned that he was coming. Then suddenly he was there. I remembered his feeling about death.

He stood in our dining-room in front of the big window.

"It is here," he said, "that I told your grandparents of the death of Henri." Regnault was killed in 1871 at the battle of Buzenval during the Siege of Paris.

"I want to see your father," Degas said.

My father was upstairs. We went to the room where his body

---

2.   Henri Regnault (1843–1871), a talented young painter, a man of extraordinary charm, a natural musician, was a friend of Bizet and Saint-Saëns, of Mallarmé and Degas. He was killed shortly before the end of the Franco-Prussian War. His best-known painting, considered revolutionary in its day, is the *Salomé* in the Metropolitan Museum in New York. Georges Clairin (1843–1920), also a painter and a close friend of Regnault's, published an edition of his letters.

was laid out. It was dark. Degas, in a loud, dictatorial voice, clamored for "Light, lots of light."

I called Francine and she opened the curtains wide. Then Degas leaned over my father's body, looking very closely at his face. He finally turned towards me and said, "This is indeed the Halévy whom we have always known with the additional grandeur that death gives. This must be kept — recorded."

He left. "This must be kept." Those words struck me. I thought of the artist Paul Renouard whose early efforts Degas had encouraged and whom my father had known through him. He lived around the corner. I found him at home. He came, worked for two hours and made a fine drawing. But it was only a fine drawing. It lacked "the grandeur that death gives." Only Degas could have captured that.

August 1910

I went to say goodbye to Degas before leaving Paris. I found him resigned, gentle, weary. He seemed pleased to see me. I told him of Cavé's death and reminded him of the way Cavé, that happy, idle dilettante, had puzzled him; of the journey to Mont-Saint-Michel, countermanded by Cavé;[3] and Degas's rage, his final judgment pronounced against Cavé, the idler. "M. Haas

3. "It had to do with an expedition to Mont-Saint-Michel which Madame Howland, Degas, and Cavé had decided to make together. Everything had been arranged including the day and time of departure. For Degas, whom it was difficult to tear away from his studio, this journey was an important matter. He looked forward to it with childlike anticipation. To Cavé, like everything else in the world, it meant nothing. Besides, he rebelled as much against engagements as he did against work; instinctively he rejected being tied down. The day before they were to leave he told Degas gently that he was 'prevented' from going. The expedition did not take place. Degas was very angry. '*Prevented*, what does that mean? You promised; you should come.' Cavé listened with a patient smile to the vehement reproaches with which Degas tried to overwhelm him. 'That's how it is, Degas. I am prevented from going.'

"For a long time Degas talked about this broken engagement; and I don't mean for weeks or for months but for years. He talked about it insistently, with that forceful repetitiousness, that wearisome

and Cavé are a pair of dancers — idlers — dancing ring-around-a-rosy."

He listened to me and smiled at his own half-forgotten remark. I think he was glad to see me again. Three days later (after I had left) he came to Sucy and stayed for dinner. It was the first time this had happened in twelve or thirteen years.

15 February 1911

I told Spire[4] about what I had written yesterday. And I repeated to him that terrible page that B—— published in a recent *Libre Entretien:* "France, a few years from now, will have lost any right to monopolize her lands, her shores; and her sterile, landowning families will be expropriated by the prolific nations."

That is the reality on which everything is based and which it is so uncomfortable to publish. They rant about the decay of one thing or another, but only one form of decay is irreparable, and that is the basis of all the others, the one they don't talk about because, they say, it is irreparable. In that case, don't talk about any of them.

I don't want to deny our moral and social disorder. Nevertheless, order has never been a French characteristic. The nation has been saved by the vitality of her peoples, the warmth of character, the abundance of individual talent. Today she is not menaced by the ever-present disorder, but by the lowering of her physical vitality, her impoverishment in manpower.

A robust country can stand the weight of bureaucracy (Russia) or an organization of corrupt politicians (the United States,

---

reiteration of which certain intense souls are capable and which was highly developed in him. Degas never tired of a friendship or a hatred, nor of an admiration, a joke or a grievance." Daniel Halévy, *Pays Parisiens.*

4. André Spire (1868–   ) was a friend of Daniel Halévy's from 1899 when they were both teaching the workmen's classes known as the *Université populaire.* "André Spire had not yet discovered the two passions of his active life: Zionism taught him by Zangwill and the technique of free verse which he studied with the Abbé Rousselot." Daniel Halévy, *Pays Parisiens.*

Italy), but when such a bureaucracy, such an organization functions in a country that is on the way down, then, then . . .

This creates an atmosphere of gloom that explains everything: the rage of Maurras, Degas's despair.

May 1911

Ingres Exhibition. I returned before it closed. It is the finest, the most triumphant exhibition I have seen; the strongest impression of the will to work, the greatest success of the solitary worker. Ingres wanted to renew style in its essential purity; and at a period that lacked nourishment from other sources, he followed a straight line, neither surprised nor weakened by being alone. What strength! What passion!

Marcel Guérin told me that Degas came the other day and stood close to the pictures. Migeon saw him and said, "Look at this."

Degas replied, "In the pictures I know I can find something, but in the ones I don't know there is nothing." And he stood in front of the canvases, touching them, running his hands over them.

June 1911

Departure of the airplanes for the European Circuit. Spent the day with young Landron who had landed in the fields between the Noiseau road and the farm road that goes straight to La Queue. His mother and two sisters were there; and Degas. He arrived alone, a blind man, feeling his way along the edge of the ditch with his cane. Florence[5] caught sight of him and helped him along. She led him around the plane. He fingered it all around. "How small it is!" he said. And suddenly, a ray of light shining on the wings enabled him to see it. "Oh, yes," he said, "it *is* very small."

Young Landron spent his last day on earth surrounded with glory and the good will of all. There were automobiles along the road offering the use of their tools; everything was his for

5. Florence was Daniel Halévy's sister-in-law, Mme Elie Halévy.

the asking. Thirty youngsters from Noiseau, from Sucy, from La Queue followed him around in a group, cheeping like a flight of sparrows. At six o'clock he was able to rise, after having controlled some rough pitching in a strong wind. He went straight into the wind towards Grosbois. Above Sucy he turned and we saw him ahead of us starting off again, this time with the wind, straight, sure of himself, a conqueror, and Quinton reassured the three women looking up at him. Half an hour later, he fell and died.

10 December 1912

Tuesday. Rouart auction. I went with Noufflard. Behind the auctioneers' stand I could see the beautiful canvases going by me, one by one.

The Louvre bought Delacroix's *l'Atelier,* Daumier's two *Scapins.* The Friends of the Luxembourg let the *Danseuses à la barre* go to Durand-Ruel for an American woman for 430,000 francs.

I had never seen a big auction. I sat facing the bidders. It was hideous: two hundred horse-dealers, speculators on the grain market, the dreariest, lowest faces. They are the merchants, the buyers. They come from Germany, from all over. In the front rows forty or so fine heads, the art-lovers: Koechlin, Metman, Blanche, Marcel Guérin. When Koechlin or Prieur bids it is a fine sight.[6]

As the sale drew to an end I heard a voice say: "Degas is here." I looked to where he was pointing and there was Degas in the little room lower down to the left, sitting motionless like a

6. Henri Rouart's collection of paintings, both ancient and modern, was one of the largest and most distinguished anywhere. The *Danseuses à la barre* was bought by Mrs. Havemeyer and is now in the Metropolitan Museum in New York.

Raymond Koechlin was one of Degas's earliest admirers. He was president of the *Société des Amis du Louvre,* and of the *Conseil des Musées Nationaux,* and author of *Ivoires gothiques français* and *Les Céramiques musulmanes de Suze.*

Marcel Guérin, critic and art collector, made a catalogue of Manet's engravings and etchings and edited Degas's letters.

blind man. I went straight over to him. They had just told him the price his picture had brought. He smiled a little as if he felt a remote kind of satisfaction.

"It's curious," he said. "Pictures I sold for five hundred francs."

I stood near him for a while. Two or three people came up, identified themselves (he can barely see). A woman who did not introduce herself greeted him, told him how much she admired him. He rose without speaking and shook her hand. Then he sat down again and said to me in a complaining voice, "Why are you wearing gloves? No hat, but gloves!" — He had said this to me twenty years ago. So I replied, "You have forgotten the remark of the mother of one of the dancers you liked so much: 'A gentleman is always nicer with his gloves on.' " "It's true," he admitted and smiled.

He stayed only a short time and left before the crowd. I rejoined him on the sidewalk of the rue de la Ville-Evèque and accompanied him. Or rather he accompanied me, walking for the sake of walking as he does these days. He talked a little, still in that distant, soft, musical voice, diminished by the burden of his eighty years.

"You are going to be quite annoyed with me," I said. (I was being cautious.) "You will find that I really belong to the tribe of writers. But I do regret that nothing has been written about Rouart's recollections of Corot, of Millet, of old Martin, the man who sold artists' supplies."

He stopped, and in that always distant voice, sad rather than complaining, as though he were repeating things remembered, he said, "Oh, literature — writers — no, what's underneath is no one's business. There must be a certain mystery. Works of art must be left with some mystery about them."

We were walking along the rue Saint-Honoré. A man stopped him, introduced himself: "M. de Moncour. I congratulate you. What a triumph!"

Degas bowed. The gentleman went on.

"What name did he say?"

"M. de Moncour, I believe."

"I don't know him, I no longer remember." And we kept on walking.

"You see," he said, "my legs are good. I walk well. But since I moved I no longer work. It's odd. I haven't put anything in order. Everything is there, leaning against the walls. I don't care. I let everything go. It's amazing how indifferent you get in old age."

We passed by the *Nouveau Cirque*.

"That was once the *bal Valentino*," he said. "One evening I unmasked a young woman there. I was at the ball; I had taken her there. I was very young then, dressed as Pierrot — I was very young."

And still we kept on walking. He steps up and down the curbstones, crosses the streets pretty well. I was constantly worried about him, but I was wrong. It is impossible to tell how much or how little he sees. He stopped all of a sudden — this was always a habit of his — as if to tell me something important. "I sleep very well," he said, "eight or nine hours a night. I can still sleep and I still have my legs."

He is not at all childish. But his higher faculties are growing numb and his time is adequately filled by mere physical processes from which he derives a sense of well-being. Nevertheless he is interested in everything — in the Balkan war, for instance — but from so far away. Always those eighty years. The distance is very long between him and us. . . .

I talk to him about Delacroix, about Corot. Did he know them? No; just met them. Ingres: he repeats the story of his visit. Valpinçon told him one day that he had just refused to loan Ingres his *Odalisque nue* (now in the Louvre) for an exhibition. Degas's rejoinder: one does not refuse M. Ingres the loan of one of his own paintings. Valpinçon, remorseful, writes a letter which Degas takes to Ingres. Ingres, standing on a ladder, climbs down, falls.

Still walking, we arrived at the Louvre. I said to Degas, "Now I know where you are going. You are going to see my mother." First he said that he was late and should take a bus home. Then: "Good heavens, I'll go up for a moment. I really want to."

He had quite forgotten the 430,000 francs. He was thinking only of the past. He stopped at the entrance to the Place Dauphine to look at the door of a house opposite where Alfred Niaudet used to live. Then he went upstairs. The children came down. Léon looked at him as though at a strange animal. He kissed Françoise[7] after remarking that she was too tall. He stayed for a little while, talking about old age; then he left.

13 December 1912
This morning the exhibition of the Rouart drawings. Degas seated in the middle of the gallery, a Homer with vacant eyes. Various young men join him from time to time.

The Prud'hons, the admirable Millets, the Delacroix, exquisite watercolors; the Corots, so upstanding. The Rousseaus, so great; Daumier: women at the theatre.

We stay half an hour until noon. Then they close the gallery and send us away. Degas goes out first and we all follow him. Is it an apotheosis or a funeral? Not out of indifference, but out of consideration everyone leaves him to his vague and grandiose solitude. He departs alone.

25 January 1913
Degas still so beautiful. The semi-absence that foretells death; and yet as soon as one speaks to him, such presence, such energy, such clarity of voice and eye.

Madame Ganderax says to him in front of his painting, "Bravo Degas! That is the Degas we love, not the Degas of the Affair."

"Madame, it is the whole Degas who wishes to be loved."

Someone asks him: "Well, you aren't unhappy with this picture, are you?"

"No, I am sure that the man who painted it is no ass; but I am convinced that whoever bought it at that price is a horse's arse."

7. Françoise Halévy is the wife of Louis Joxe, who has played an important rôle in the DeGaulle government as Ambassador to Russia and in Algerian affairs.

111

Someone else congratulates him on the price. "I am a race-horse," he says. "I run the long races, but I am satisfied with my bag of oats."

1916

I hear that Degas is ill — the bronchial tubes as always. He now lives in a new apartment in the Boulevard des Batignolles. I go there. It is my first visit. One of his nieces who has come to nurse him opens the door and takes me to his room. It is a bare room, new, with no past. Degas, immobile in bed, greets me with a kind word or two. I sit down on a chair. No conversation.

At a given moment the niece comes and straightens the pillow. Her short sleeve is transparent. All of a sudden Degas seizes her arm in both hands with more strength than one would have believed possible. He places her right arm in the light that shines from the window. He looks at it with passionate concentration. How many women's arms he has looked at like this and, so to speak, spied on in the light of his studio. I had been thinking that his strength was exhausted, but here he was, still working.

November 1917

The very night before my orders came Degas died. In the evening I went to his apartment. I looked at him for a long time and remembered far back. Oh, the kindness of this mask, idealized by old age, emaciated by illness, calmed by death. The long hair, the long beard — a Christ, throughout my childhood — but between then and now how much has happened: fifteen, twenty years of separation from this man, and life since, my life, which has not lived up to the magnificent, loving examples I was given as a child.

The next morning my orders come to report to the Saxe barracks. I go there and am given orders to leave for Nantes. I go to the office and ask for a delay. I need it for my *Wilson*.[8] Then

8. Daniel Halévy was at this time working on a life of Woodrow Wilson.

Degas about 1910.
Photograph attributed to Sacha Guitry.

Courtesy of Bibliothèque Nationale.

Daniel Halévy in his late eighties.
Courtesy of Madame Joxe.

home, a quick lunch with Mama and Léon, and we go to the funeral.

Few people in the church, but why should there be more? The Rouarts, Mademoiselle Cassatt (I believe), Bartholomé, some old men, Vollard, Renouard — a hundred people at most.[9] ... The music is beautiful, moving, but the real emotion lies in death itself. The ritual music that absorbs one's thought, that mirrors eternity is moving, but it dilutes the true, the shocking significance of death. When the clergy withdraws, when the organ is silent and the body in the coffin remains alone, surrounded by friends, then nothing is left but death, the snatching away, the destruction, the end.

Poor children who die alone on the field of battle, crying out in pain, with no woman's voice, no hand to touch, you know what death is. Poor Degas, so much loved, here all alone. A corpse, poor flesh that quivers in the coffin when the pallbearers carry it away! We surround him, we follow him, we put him in the ground. —

That stone lies heavily on my past.

2 May 1918

Monday I went to Durand-Ruel's. All of Degas's studio is there, all the paintings that could be easily moved. They were shifting them around, comparing them — the early ones that he had saved, and all the unfinished ones of the last years. The in-between period is lacking, but that was not the most valuable. Degas's studies are admirable, and admirable, too, the forms that grew out of his despair, the colors he smeared, crushing the pastel onto the canvas, to rest from what had become for him the exhausting work of perceiving form. Marcel Guérin was there, Raymond Koechlin, Metman, Vollard. . . . We stayed from five to seven, handling these extraordinary works, so violent, so sad.

9. Among others who attended the funeral were Claude Monet, Jean Bérard, Forain, José-Maria Sert, Raffaëlli, J. and G. Durand-Ruel.

Saturday [n.d.]

Degas exhibition at Petit's. Pastels, portraits fill the gallery — at the end the family portrait the Louvre has bought; Mlle Fiocre in the ballet *La Source;* ten or more early paintings; and hanging on the partitions, pastels and drawings in the late manner, heavily, brutally drawn: women in their baths, dancers, women combing their hair, women reclining, thighs spread; a collection of experiments, striking discoveries, but carried out with a kind of relentless pursuit into the depths of ugliness; surprising, depressing depths. In the first of the small galleries at the left of the stairs are the drawings and studies for *Sémiramis, The Young Spartans, The Martyrdom of the City of Orléans,* the most clear-cut, the most elegant forms, an intense awareness of the beauty, the dignity of the human body which was so harshly degraded in the late works. . . . What a strange story this *oeuvre* tells!

The extremely large public is astonished and dares show it, which is unusual. They consider the forms coarse, the pastels a complete mystery. His experiments embody the pursuit of a truth that doesn't interest them. A nice woman standing next to me said, "And to think they couldn't raise 400,000 francs for Regnault's *Salomé.*"

The stupefaction of the public seems to me rational; what seems irrational is this chain of influence, of snobbism, of financial interests and speculations which through publicity in the press reaches people who feel almost obliged to come to see these works created in a world apart by an extraordinary man who asked nothing more of them than peace in which to work. Suddenly I recalled vividly the familiar figure of Degas, standing in his studio, with his long hair, his shaggy beard. "How simple it would be," he used to say, "if they would just leave us alone. The journalists bore the public with our works and annoy us with their articles, their comments. Always they want to explain; they're forever explaining. There *is* nothing to explain. How stupid to make people come and see what we are doing — Beauty is a mystery." He spoke with no violence, rather with desolation — a dirty, disheveled, sordid Prospero in his studio filled with bizarre sculpture, shriveled wax figures crumbling into dust, and unfinished, unwrapped canvases leaning against the wall in sad disorder. He lived like that in the dirt and the dark, handling his canvases, turning them over and over, until fatigue and an overwhelming indifference invaded his spirit and deadened his will-power. He died in this state of indifference, in poverty, on the fifth floor of the tall house where he had lived far away among his drawings and canvases.

In the gallery one of his paintings stood on an easel facing the daylight; it was the young boys and girls preparing to fight — the tense, elegant young bodies forming such a simple, such a free composition. I had looked at it for a long while the first time I saw it, when Degas explained it to me: "It is young Spartan girls challenging the boys to combat," and I think he added, "I read about it in Plutarch."

Now I see it here, surrounded by all the studies I hadn't known; framed together, two sepia sketches as clear-cut and pure as in a notebook of Poussin's. And the drawings, too: one splendid young girl, in profile, her left arm taut.

In the next little room I met Elémir Bourges stopping in front of a late pastel, a ballet dancer bending over with no grace at all. I spoke to him, this old master of the 1880's. His head emerged from a vast muffler, pale and cadaverous. Young people came up and greeted him. He is respected, and he merits it, this author of three carefully executed novels who, counter to the current of realism, has maintained a sense of imagination and literary composition. Actually he has lived against his time, which is no doubt one of the reasons for his lack of success. I approached him without knowing what impression Degas's work made on him. But as soon as he started speaking he exploded. He was aroused, irritated by this display of willful, deliberate, repetitious ugliness, by these formless sketches. In vain I tried to point out to him the passion that emerges from this work, a passion for the right design, for the sharpest foreshortening, a pursuit of form, of modeling, of color, which from among so many experiments produces such magnificent results. Elémir

Bourges was not appeased. The more intense the assault on beauty in the work, the more indignant he became; in addition he resented this energy gone astray. I listened, I admitted the singularity of the work. Degas himself was the first to feel it, and that was the reason for the secrecy in which he lived. I admitted that there is destruction, catastrophe in this work and to explain it I told him of the eye trouble which from 1870 on interfered with Degas's work, prevented his making large-scale designs, forced him to work in fragments, always contending with semi-darkness.[1]

Elémir Bourges listened, admitted this, then said, "Doubtless to understand these modern artists it is necessary to know their physiology." I found it indulgent of him to admit this. For although the accident of his loss of sight can explain Degas's renunciation of large compositions and the study of detail, it does not explain the moral change in his work, the retrogression of inspiration. Yes, there is catastrophe in this work, as there is in the whole history of French art after 1870. But in this catastrophe no one was greater than Degas, no one drew more magnificent results from despair.[2]

14 November 1930

I went to see Forain.

It was about Degas's letters. Did he have any? He lives at Versailles and comes to Paris every afternoon to work in the rue Spontini.

So here I am in the rue Spontini. A disorderly studio. Some sketches for paintings. On the mantelpiece as well-known thirteenth-century French sculpture. That woman wearing a *coiffe,* a woman of thirty with such a lifelike face, the ghost of a smile

1. I must point out that on page 22 of this very book I gave a wholly different explanation of the disaster that affected Degas's work. D.H.

2. This somewhat surprising point of view is perhaps explained by the permanent influence on M. Halévy's thinking of Renan who once remarked to Ludovic Halévy, "One must admit that it is good to live in periods of decadence."

on her thin lips, her shoulder bent forward a little, her arm bent. . . . I recognized her, but I don't know her origin or what she is called.

Forain comes in, a shrunken, exhausted old man. Where is the tall, muscular bounder I used to see at my aunt's house around 1896 before the Dreyfus Affair?[3]

"I was seventy-nine three days ago," he said. "Those three days count . . . I am very tired."

"But you are working, you still produce . . ."

"I still have a few good days."

I remind him of the object of my visit. Degas. He had not forgotten.

Looking straight at me, he says, "Degas liked you very much. I know that the Affair separated you. But during the Affair I often heard him say 'My poor Halévys . . .' "

For the moment I felt as though he had let me come just to tell me that. He had no letters, he said, just some notes, too trivial to be published.

Perhaps it wasn't exactly for that reason he had me come, but certainly it was primarily to talk about Degas. I was sure he didn't regret it. From the outset we found ourselves on a singular basis of equality and confidence. To have known a man like Degas creates a bond, almost an intimacy. Actually each of us is touched on his deepest level and relives the past. But "touched" is not the right word; it says too little. This intimacy which we rediscovered in ourselves was invoked, almost created by Degas. What we revive, our meeting ground is Degas himself. . . .

"Everything I am," Forain said, "I owe to him. Fifty years

3. "Let us admit at once our admiration for the artist so we can add without delay the full horror with which the man inspires us." "Les Carnets intimes de Robert de Montesquiou," *Les Nouvelles littéraires*, July 21, 1928. This remark by Maurice Barrès about Forain is quoted in Montesquiou's notebooks.

Forain was an anti-Dreyfusard who, in spite of the fact that Madame Straus had been one of his most helpful patrons, ceased going to her house at the time of the Dreyfus Affair.

ago I indulged in a little anarchy. Four or five words from him were sufficient warning."

"Well," I said, "since you have told me this I will follow your lead and say that the best of myself I owe to him. Two or three times a week he came for lunch. What conversation! Throughout my youth I heard it. But he never taught me to put art on a pedestal."

Whereupon Forain remembered an example of that austere humor, that severe judgment of art, so typical of Degas.

"It was during the war — 1870 — Tissot, James Tissot, the one who illustrated the Bible for Hachette. He met Degas somewhere, told him that Cavelier (a sculptor) had been seriously wounded at Le Bourget, that he had seen him. 'I did a drawing of him — here, look.' Degas forcibly pushed away the sketch, refusing to look at it. 'You would have done better if you'd picked him up,' he said."

And Forain, delighted, repeated the remark, acting out again the forceful gesture of Degas's arm. How well he would once have drawn it.

"Ah, the things he said," Forain continued. "I remember some trouble we once had about a dancer who posed for us and was hired away by a rich amateur. At his place there was port wine, there were cakes, all sorts of things we didn't give her. Degas was very cross. One evening we met this amateur at the opera and Degas told him what he thought of him: 'Monsieur, you have no right to deprive us of our tools.' "

"Yes," I said, "the typical remark of an artisan. And you know he liked working people, understood them wonderfully, appreciated their speech when it was good. I remember his delight when he returned from a journey in Touraine. He told us of a remark . . ."

"Yes, yes," Forain interrupted happily. "It was what a shoemaker said when he had given a drink to the dog that was with Degas and his friends. Degas wanted to give him a tip and he wouldn't accept it. 'Monsieur,' he said, 'you would not want me to take your money for the sip of milk I gave your dog.' Oh, those remarks of Degas, the shortcuts he found. One day he said to me,

'There is a kind of success that is indistinguishable from panic.' "

I had not heard that one which is indeed superb. For both ruin and certain kinds of success result from a loss of common sense to which we are all subject.

Forain repeated to me an opinion of Degas on modern painting. It had to do with the Nativity. "What wonderful subjects!" Degas said. "And how unfortunate it is that we have let them be appropriated by imbeciles."

"That was an idea he often had," I said, and recalled a remark that Forain did not know about women in tubs and Susanna and the Elders. — " 'To think that in another age I would have been painting Susanna and the Elders.' I still remember the affection he had in his old age for the early canvas that he had placed on an easel — *Spartan Girls Challenging Spartan Boys to Combat.*"

Whereupon Forain added, "He once said to me, 'It needs a group of pregnant women watching.' "

What a beautiful idea! I can see now how he would have tried to give all its meaning, all its significance to that line of the bellies, so neglected by painters except for a few of the Dutch. As to Degas's persistent preference and regret for the painting of the past, I told Forain that he would find an apt expression of it in the letters we have collected. He wrote to Bartholomé, "My heart is withered. I have locked it away in a pink ballet slipper. . . ."[4]

We chatted some more, about a certain violence in Degas, his hatred of flowers, his faithful friendships ("He saw your father again on his deathbed, didn't he?" Forain asked, and I told him about the visit, Degas's order to pull back the curtains and open the blinds. Forain listened attentively), about the law-suit brought against the heirs of one brother by the brothers in New

4. His exact words, written January 17, 1886, were, "I speak of the past because except for my heart every part of me seems to be aging all at once. And there is even something artificial about my heart. The dancers sewed it up in a pink satin bag, a slightly faded pink satin like their ballet slippers." *Lettres de Degas.*

119

Orleans. (I had not known the dramatic episode in which the lawyer arrived the very day the brother died, declaring to the children who neither knew nor understood anything about it, that he claimed the right to attach the property of the deceased. "There is someone here who will understand me," the lawyer said and pointed to an old housekeeper who had come from New Orleans with the dead brother when he returned to France. The lawyer took her aside for a moment. Then she turned to the children of the dead man and said, "Everything this man says is true.")

We talked, too, of what Degas was like during the 1914 war. "Far away," Forain said. It was the right phrase. He seemed to be away, far, far away from things. Yet he was not unaware of the war. When Forain told him one day that he was part of a camouflage team Degas said, "That is very honorable," and fell silent. Forain admired the fitness of the word, and of the emphasis Degas gave to the word "honorable." We talked about Degas's funeral. There were so few of us. "That day," Forain said, "I had an argument with Bartholomé. He had told Poincaré about the funeral and arranged for the appearance of a representative of the President. Would Degas have wanted that?" Forain told me too of a remark that Degas made to Bartholomé that astonished me, for Degas was very fond of him.

"Bartholomé," he said, "you will be like Guillaume" (Guillaume, the academic sculptor, a cousin of the Rouarts, a widower like Bartholomé) "with your tear-filled eyes gazing up at the heavens, you will round up plenty of honors and decorations. . . ." Forain accompanied me to the door, showing me on the staircase a First Empire canvas he had just bought and two heads painted by his wife.

15 December 1930

Saw Forain again yesterday. Tragic in his extreme old age — coughing, spitting.

"It's nothing," he said. "The emphysema is better. Now it's my heart. After working for seventy-eight years it is now kept going by inoculations. However, I shall be able to go back to work. I want to finish that."

He pointed out one of his canvases, a Christ standing, doubtless going to his trial. Tired eyes, face drawn, but there is energy in the set of the lips.

Forain is still happy, eager to talk about Degas.

"Did I tell you about his reconciliation with Manet?" he asked.

"No. I never knew they quarreled."

"Oh, yes. They didn't speak for three or four years. Manet liked practical jokes. Degas didn't. Manet and some others thought that Degas slept with his maid. They questioned her and started her talking. She said, 'Monsieur? No. He is not a man. I once went in his room when he was changing his shirt and he said to me, "Get out, you miserable creature!" ' So there was a quarrel. Then after three or four years an intermediary arranged for Degas to go to Manet's studio to see his work. Degas looked at sketches, at pastels. He didn't talk much, said that his eyes were tired, that he couldn't see well. A few days later Manet ran into a friend who told him, 'I met Degas the other day as he was coming out of your studio. He was enthusiastic, bowled over by everything you showed him.' 'Oh, the pig,' Manet replied. 'He said absolutely nothing to me.' "

Finally I left Forain. He hadn't found the letters from Degas.

"Ah, Degas," he said. "How handsome he was in the end, walking through the streets — "

"Yes, wasn't he? In his Inverness cape, tapping his cane, feeling his way. Yet he walked quickly, always alone. . . . How extraordinary is the magic of greatness. It shows in every step. . . ."

My Friend Degas : Index of Names

MINA CURTISS, sometime associate professor of English at Smith College, is well known as editor-translator of *The Letters of Marcel Proust* and author of *Bizet and his World*. Her copious notes to the present volume are based as frequently as possible on M. Halévy's autobiographical *Pays Parisiens* and on Degas's published letters. These notes, setting the stage and supplying background of many persons and events unfamiliar to American readers, reflect the editor's long and close concern with the world of French arts and letters in perhaps its richest period.

Of the sixteen photographs in this book, six were taken by Degas himself and six more were posed by him but taken by other hands. They come from the personal collection of Mme. Louis Joxe, M. Halévy's daughter, and from that given to the Bibliothèque Nationale by M. Jean Nepveu-Degas. The self-portrait on the front of the jacket is reproduced by courtesy of M. Nepveu-Degas.